SO-AHJ-544

COMPACT *Research*

Teen Smoking

Current Issues

ReferencePoint Press®

San Diego, CA

Select* books in the Compact Research series include:

Current Issues

Abortion
Animal Experimentation
Biomedical Ethics
Cloning
Conflict in the Middle East
The Death Penalty
Energy Alternatives
Free Speech
Genetic Engineering
Global Warming and
    Climate Change
Gun Control
Illegal Immigration

Islam
Media Violence
National Security
Nuclear Weapons and
    Security
Obesity
School Violence
Stem Cells
Terrorist Attacks
U.S. Border Control
Video Games
World Energy Crisis

Diseases and Disorders

ADHD
Alzheimer's Disease
Anorexia
Autism
Bipolar Disorders
Hepatitis

HPV
Meningitis
Phobias
Sexually Transmitted
    Diseases

Drugs

Alcohol
Antidepressants
Club Drugs
Cocaine and Crack
Hallucinogens
Heroin
Inhalants

Marijuana
Methamphetamine
Nicotine and Tobacco
Performance-Enhancing
    Drugs
Prescription Drugs
Steroids

Energy and the Environment

Biofuels
Deforestation
Hydrogen Power

Solar Power
Wind Power

*For a complete list of titles please visit www.referencepointpress.com.

COMPACT *Research*

Teen Smoking

by Lydia D. Bjornlund

Current Issues

ReferencePoint
Press®

San Diego, CA

For more information, contact:
ReferencePoint Press, Inc.
PO Box 27779
San Diego, CA 92198
www.ReferencePointPress.com

Picture credits:
Cover: Dreamstime and iStockphoto.com
Maury Aaseng: 32–34, 48–50, 64–67, 80–83
AP Images: 17
iStockphoto.com: 12

LIBRARY OF CONGRESS CATALOGING-IN-PUBLICATION DATA

Bjornlund, Lydia D.
  Teen smoking / by Lydia D. Bjornlund.
    p. cm. — (Compact research series)
  Includes bibliographical references and index.
  ISBN-13: 978-1-60152-098-2 (hardback)
  ISBN-10: 1-60152-098-0 (hardback)
  1. Teenagers—Tobacco use—United States. 2. Smoking—United States. 3. Tobacco use—United States—Prevention. I. Title.
  HV5745.B55 2009
  362.29'608350973—dc22
                                                    2009028008

Contents

Foreword

As modern civilization continues to evolve, its ability to create, store, distribute, and access information expands exponentially. The explosion of information from all media continues to increase at a phenomenal rate. By 2020 some experts predict the worldwide information base will double every 73 days. While access to diverse sources of information and perspectives is paramount to any democratic society, information alone cannot help people gain knowledge and understanding. Information must be organized and presented clearly and succinctly in order to be understood. The challenge in the digital age becomes not the creation of information, but how best to sort, organize, enhance, and present information.

ReferencePoint Press developed the *Compact Research* series with this challenge of the information age in mind. More than any other subject area today, researching current issues can yield vast, diverse, and unqualified information that can be intimidating and overwhelming for even the most advanced and motivated researcher. The *Compact Research* series offers a compact, relevant, intelligent, and conveniently organized collection of information covering a variety of current topics ranging from illegal immigration and deforestation to diseases such as anorexia and meningitis.

The series focuses on three types of information: objective single-author narratives, opinion-based primary source quotations, and facts and statistics. The clearly written objective narratives provide context and reliable background information. Primary source quotes are carefully selected and cited, exposing the reader to differing points of view. And facts and statistics sections aid the reader in evaluating perspectives. Presenting these key types of information creates a richer, more balanced learning experience.

For better understanding and convenience, the series enhances information by organizing it into narrower topics and adding design features that make it easy for a reader to identify desired content. For example, in *Compact Research: Illegal Immigration*, a chapter covering the economic impact of illegal immigration has an objective narrative explaining the various ways the economy is impacted, a balanced section of numerous primary source quotes on the topic, followed by facts and full-color illustrations to encourage evaluation of contrasting perspectives.

The ancient Roman philosopher Lucius Annaeus Seneca wrote, "It is quality rather than quantity that matters." More than just a collection of content, the *Compact Research* series is simply committed to creating, finding, organizing, and presenting the most relevant and appropriate amount of information on a current topic in a user-friendly style that invites, intrigues, and fosters understanding.

Teen Smoking at a Glance

Prevalence

More than 3.5 million U.S. high school students—roughly 20 percent of the total—smoke cigarettes; about 11.6 percent of high school seniors smoke daily.

Trends

A smaller proportion of teens smoke today than ever. The U.S. rate of teen smoking peaked in the mid-1990s, when half of teens had tried a cigarette and more than one-third of teens smoked regularly.

Adults Who Smoked as Teens

More than 80 percent of current adult smokers began before the age of 18.

Health Dangers

Tobacco use is the cause of one in five deaths annually in the United States—more deaths than HIV, illegal drug use, alcohol use, motor vehicle injuries, suicides, and murders combined.

Secondhand Smoke

Nonsmoking adults who are exposed to secondhand smoke increase their risk of heart disease by 25–30 percent and their risk of lung cancer by 20–30 percent.

Costs to Society

The Centers for Disease Control and Prevention (CDC) estimates that smokers cost the United States $96 billion a year in direct health care costs and an additional $97 billion a year in lost productivity.

Advertising Restrictions

Tobacco companies in the United States have been prohibited from targeting children and teens in advertising, marketing, and promotions since 1998. Subsequent legislation has strengthened these prohibitions.

Tobacco Control

All 50 states, the District of Columbia, and the 5 U.S. territories have laws that make it illegal to sell tobacco products to minors, or someone who is under the age of 18. The minimum age of purchase is 19 in 4 states (as of 2009).

Access

More than three-quarters of teens under 18 say it is easy to obtain cigarettes and other tobacco products.

Oversight

The 2009 Family Smoking Prevention and Tobacco Control Act gave the U.S. Food and Drug Administration (FDA) oversight of the tobacco industry. One of the goals of this legislation was to strengthen youth prevention measures.

Attitudes Toward Smoking

Over 75 percent of high school seniors say that they prefer to date people who do not smoke, and nearly two-thirds say that becoming a smoker reflects poor judgment. Almost 90 percent disapprove of teens smoking one or more packs of cigarettes a day.

Prevention

Programs that combine school-based prevention activities with complementary mass media or community programs can reduce teen smoking by 20 percent.

Quitting

The vast majority of teens who smoke are nicotine-dependent; almost half of current teen smokers have already tried to quit.

Overview

> **❝I know how difficult it can be to break this habit [of smoking] when it's been with you for a long time. And I also know that kids today don't just start smoking for no reason. They're aggressively targeted as customers by the tobacco industry.❞**
>
> —President Barack Obama, at the June 2009 signing of the Family Smoking Prevention and Tobacco Control Act.

> **❝I know smoking may be dangerous, but I still do it. Because I don't think it's quite as dangerous as they want us all to believe. I know many smokers who have smoked for over 50 years and had no ill health effects.❞**
>
> —Bill Williams, founder of SmokingLobby.com, an online forum and advocacy group protecting the rights of smokers.

According to the U.S. Department of Health and Human Services, cigarette smoking is the leading preventable cause of death in the United States. An estimated 443,000 Americans die prematurely as a result of smoking or exposure to secondhand smoke. This total exceeds the death toll of HIV/AIDS, substance abuse, motor vehicle collisions, suicide, and homicide combined. Government health agencies estimate that smoking accounts for serious illness in another 8.6 million Americans.

Because nicotine is so addictive, it is difficult for most people to quit smoking once they have begun. For this reason, health experts are particularly concerned about stopping people from starting to smoke in the first place. Studies have shown that, for the most part, people who do not use tobacco when they are teens never start. In addition, the younger people are when they begin smoking, the more likely they are to develop long-term nicotine addiction and be unable to quit as adults.

For these reasons, many antismoking efforts focus on young people. In 2000 the Department of Health and Human Services established a national health objective for 2010 to reduce cigarette use among high school students to 16 percent or less. Teen smoking has declined since this report was issued, but just a year before the 2010 deadline, the rate remains over 20 percent. The Centers for Disease Control and Prevention (CDC) has called for communitywide comprehensive tobacco-control programs to achieve the 2010 objective.

How Serious a Problem Is Teen Smoking?

Studies indicate that 1 out of 5 eighth graders has tried cigarettes, and 1 in 15 smokes on a regular basis. By the time they are seniors in high school, roughly half have tried cigarettes. One in 5 high school seniors is a regular smoker (smoking at least 1 cigarette in a month), over 1 in 10 smoke daily, and 1 in 20 smokes half a pack of cigarettes or more daily. Although most of these teens do not consider themselves lifelong smokers, experts warn that most of them will become physically addicted and be unable to quit. As many as 90 percent of teens who smoke today will still be smoking in 25 years.

> " An estimated 443,000 Americans die prematurely as a result of smoking or exposure to secondhand smoke. "

While health professionals are alarmed about how many young people use tobacco products, research shows that fewer teens smoke today than in the past. Some researchers take this as a sign of hope for the future. According to the *Monitoring the Future* survey, an annual survey that charts alcohol, tobacco, and drug use by eighth-, tenth-, and twelfth-grade students, "by 2008, cigarette use [had] reached the lowest levels recorded in the life of the study, going back 33 years in the case of 12th graders."[1] Still, the declines have not always been steady, and antismoking advocates emphasize that continued progress will require ongoing advocacy and vigilance.

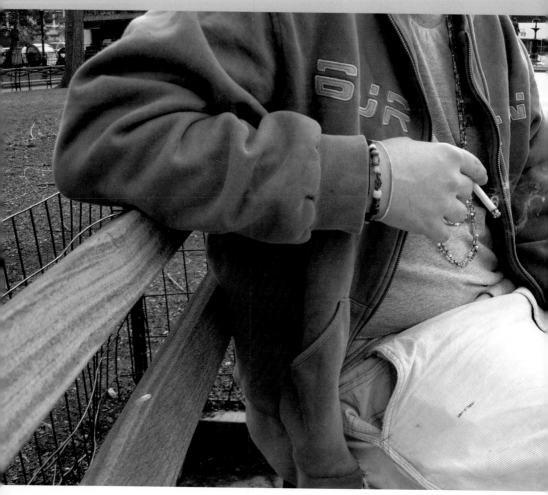

Despite recent declines in teen smoking, studies show that more than 20 percent of American teens smoke. According to those studies, 1 in 20 high school seniors smokes half a pack of cigarettes or more every day and 1 in 10 smokes at least once a day.

Who Are Teen Smokers?

Teen smokers come from all races and backgrounds. A higher percentage of teenage boys use tobacco products than do girls, but cigarette smoking rates for high school boys and girls are roughly the same. More boys than girls smoke cigars, however, and the use of smokeless tobacco products is almost exclusively a male behavior.

In general, more white than black or Hispanic teens use tobacco. For instance, the CDC's 2007 Youth Risk Behavior survey indicates that the smoking rate for white students (23.2 percent) was twice that of black students (11.6 percent) and much more than Hispanic students (16.7 percent). Interestingly, little difference was found among the rates for trying cigarettes.

Smoking rates are higher for children of one or more parents who smoke cigarettes. Teens who have friends or siblings who smoke or who have more favorable attitudes toward smoking are more likely to smoke than those who do not. This may be due in part to the fact that these teens have greater access to cigarettes. Smoking among teens, as well as adults, occurs in greater proportions among groups of low socioeconomic status and low levels of academic achievement.

Unlike many other risky teen behaviors, prevalence of teen cigarette use varies greatly from one state to another. The CDC report concludes, "These variations might occur, in part, because of differences in state and local laws and policies, enforcement practices, access to illegal drugs, availability of effective school and community interventions, prevailing behavioral and social norms, demographic characteristics of the population, and adult practices."[2]

Why Teens Smoke

Teens use tobacco products for many reasons. Many teens smoke because it makes them feel older or more confident or because they think smoking a cigarette or cigar makes them look "cool." Others smoke cigarettes to be part of a group. Most teens try their first cigarette in the presence of a good friend. This shared experience can make teen smokers feel closer.

Some young people are lured by the functional benefits of tobacco. They might smoke because they think it helps them to stay thin, keeps them alert, or helps them to relax. Cigarettes and smokeless tobacco products also can help teens act tougher than they feel. Rebellious teens are sometimes attracted to things simply because they are forbidden. The idea that they are going against their

> " Unlike many other risky teen behaviors, prevalence of teen cigarette use varies greatly from one state to another. "

parents or other authority figures can be alluring. Some teens might enjoy the excitement of trying to hide their smoking.

Many young people do not fully appreciate the health risks of smoking. They reckon that a few cigarettes will not hurt them and assume they can quit before they are addicted. Once teens start smoking, it can be hard to quit. Like adults, they begin to use cigarettes as a crutch—to help them relax or deal with stressful situations. The nicotine in cigarettes is highly addictive. Teens may quickly move from smoking on occasion to daily use.

What Today's Teens Smoke

Cigarettes are the favored form of tobacco use among teens. Today, about 20 percent of high school students smoke cigarettes. Compared to adults, teens tend to prefer name brands of cigarettes. Roughly 80 percent of teen smokers use Marlboro or Camel cigarettes, whereas 40 percent of adult smokers prefer generic brands.

The second most prevalent form of tobacco among teens is cigars. In 2007, 13.6 percent of high school students reported in the *Monitoring the Future* study that they had smoked one or more cigars in the previous 30 days.

Roughly 1 in every 15 seniors in high school smokes kreteks, a clove cigarette that is popular in Indonesia. Another trend is bidi cigarettes, or "beadies." Considered a poor person's cigarette in India, where they are common, bidis come in several flavors and cost just half the price of cigarettes in the United States. Nationwide more than 13 percent of teens have tried bidis, and experts worry that use is increasing. In addition to the taste, part of the appeal of kretek and bidi cigarettes is that young people mistakenly assume they are safer than other types of cigarettes.

How Widespread Is the Use of Smokeless Tobacco?

Almost 8 percent of high school students—and 12 percent of high school seniors—use smokeless tobacco—either snuff or chewing tobacco. Almost all smokeless tobacco is used by boys. About one-third of the users of smokeless tobacco are under age 21; more than half of these users developed the habit before they were 13.

Many terms are used to describe smokeless tobacco: spit, chewing tobacco, chaw, and snuff. The main difference is the size of the blocks. Chewing tobacco usually comes in strands or cakes. Snuff is more finely ground and comes in cans or pouches. Manufacturers add sugar to the tobacco in most of these products to improve their taste. Some are also flavored with licorice, salt, cloves, allspice, wintergreen, or other flavorings. With all of these smokeless products, users take a "pinch" and place it between the lip or cheek and gum. Some teens begin with "dip" products that do not contain any nicotine. Usually, teens who use these products at some point move on to traditional chewing tobacco or snuff.

How Today's Teen Smoking Rates Compare with Past Rates

In the 1940s and 1950s, smoking was seen as a normal thing to do. Few people—at least outside of the tobacco companies—were aware of the serious health ramifications. In fact, some advertisements touted the health benefits of smoking a cigarette or pipe. The first changes to these attitudes—and to smoking rates—occurred in the 1960s, when the U.S. surgeon general issued a report about the dangers of smoking.

In the coming decades, health professionals began to become increasingly proactive about reducing the amount of smoking, particularly among young people, and researchers began tracking how many teens were using tobacco.

In the mid-1990s attorneys general of 46 states brought a lawsuit against the major tobacco companies, charging them with lying to the public about known dangers of smoking. In 1998 the tobacco companies settled this major lawsuit out of court in an agreement known as the Master Settlement Agreement (MSA). The negative publicity that resulted from the case, as well as the changes in marketing brought about by the agreement, contributed to declining smoking rates among both teens and adults.

> " **In general, more teens today than in the past believe that serious risks are involved with smoking and express general disapproval of cigarettes.** "

By the end of the first decade of the twenty-first century, teen smoking rates were lower than ever. In 2008, according to the *Monitoring the Future* study, just 11.4 percent of high school seniors reported daily use of cigarettes, compared to 22.4 percent in 1998. In addition, fewer students today try smoking than in the past. In the 2008 study, 21 percent of eighth graders said they had tried a cigarette, down from a high of 49 percent in 1996.

Attitudes toward smoking have changed as well. In general, more teens today than in the past believe that serious risks are involved with smoking and express general disapproval of cigarettes. Three-quarters of high school seniors say that they prefer to date people who do not smoke, and nearly two-thirds said they agreed with the statement that "becoming a smoker reflects poor judgment."[3]

Studies on the trends regarding teen use of smokeless tobacco products—dip, chewing tobacco, and snuff—are inconclusive. Some studies show that the use of smokeless tobacco products has declined since the mid-1990s, but others show a gradual increase in these products, particularly among high school boys—a trend that researchers think may be in response to antismoking campaigns that fail to include smokeless tobacco products.

The Consequences of Teen Smoking

Smoking has been shown to be harmful to one's health. The American Lung Association reports that 87 percent of lung cancer cases are the direct result of smoking. In addition to lung cancer, tobacco use causes cancers of the mouth, throat, esophagus, kidneys, stomach, and bladder. According to the American Cancer Society, "Smoking damages nearly every organ in the human body, is linked to at least 15 different cancers, and accounts for some 30 percent of all cancer deaths."[4]

Smoking cigarettes also causes emphysema, a disease in which the tiny air sacs in the lungs are damaged, making it difficult for oxygen to pass from the lungs into the bloodstream. Some smokers also suffer from chronic bronchitis, an irritation and inflammation of the airways in the lungs.

Smoking has a more immediate impact as well. Because it reduces air flow to the lungs, it is difficult for smokers to compete in sports. Smokers are more susceptible than nonsmokers to colds, flu, and other illnesses,

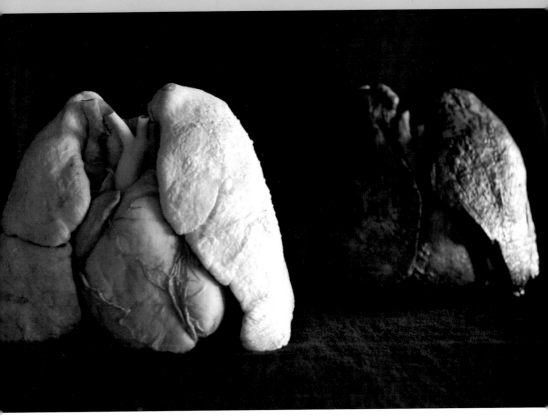

Healthy human lungs, left, are pink, spongy, and elastic. A smoker's lungs, right, are blackened and diseased.

and recovery time is slower. Emergency room data indicate that smokers require hospital treatment much more often than nonsmokers.

Some antismoking advocates also warn that social problems can result from smoking. Smokers tend to be less successful at school and engage more often in other risky behaviors, such as alcohol and drug use. Teen smokers also have higher incidences of depression as adults. Experts disagree, however, about whether smoking is a contributing factor to these problems or whether in fact it is these problems that tempt a teen to begin smoking.

Who Is to Blame for Teen Smoking?

Many people believe that the blame for teen smoking can and should be placed squarely on the shoulders of the tobacco industry. Tobacco companies spend billions of dollars on marketing. Antismoking advocates say that a key goal of the marketing campaigns is to attract new smokers to replace those who have quit or died. Since the vast majority of people start smoking before they are 19 or 20, they say, cigarette manufacturers naturally focus on attracting young smokers. They point to the addition of candy flavorings, for instance, as well as colorful packaging that they believe is meant to attract the attention of children and teens.

The tobacco companies vehemently deny accusations that they are trying to attract underage smokers—a strategy that was made illegal by the 1998 Master Settlement Agreement. They say that their advertising and marketing campaigns are intended to increase brand awareness among current adult smokers, not to attract teens. In addition, they say they have enacted a host of programs designed to restrict sales of tobacco products to minors.

> " Many people believe that the blame for teen smoking can and should be placed squarely on the shoulders of the tobacco industry. "

Clearly other factors impact a child's decision about whether to take up smoking. Self-image may play a role, as well as family and friends. Many studies suggest that parents play a significant role in whether children and teens choose to smoke. Children with parents who talk to them about the dangers of smoking are less likely to smoke than children whose parents are silent on this topic. In addition, smoking is less prevalent among children and teens whose parents are active participants in their lives. The most important influence, however, is whether one or more parents smoke cigarettes. Studies suggest that children of parents who smoke have a 50 percent greater chance of becoming smokers themselves.

How Should Teen Smoking Be Regulated?

Successfully addressing teen smoking requires addressing both supply and demand. All 50 states address supply by prohibiting the sale of tobacco products to minors. In addition, some states have enacted legislation to further restrict the supply of tobacco to minors. Examples of laws include raising the minimum age for cigarette sales, making it illegal for an adult to purchase cigarettes for a minor, banning cigarette vending machines, and requiring cigarette displays to be behind the counter.

Antismoking advocates say addressing demand for tobacco products requires laws that restrict advertising campaigns that make smoking look appealing. Antismoking organizations say this will require eliminating smoking from movies, television, and other media, as well as banning advertising and marketing by the tobacco industry. Freedom of speech advocates say that bans on depictions of smoking violate the First Amendment rights guaranteed by the Constitution. Others say that it is simply unrealistic to expect to shield children and teens from all depictions of smoking because smoking is a part of real life.

Because smoking is viewed as a public health risk, laws restricting cigarette advertising have been viewed as constitutional. The MSA prohibits targeting children and teens in advertising, marketing, and promotions of tobacco products. More recent legislation has strengthened the prohibitions of marketing strategies that may appeal to youth, including prohibiting advertising in teen magazines, outdoor billboards, and advertising within 1,000 yards of schools.

Current Laws

Laws governing cigarette sales are not always effective. Research shows that the vast majority of teens get their cigarettes from retailers rather than from friends or family members. Clerks at convenience stores, gas stations, supermarkets, and other venues have historically been lax about requiring ID for cigarette purchases. In response to evidence that states were not effectively enforcing laws prohibiting the sale of cigarettes to minors, Congress passed the Synar Amendment in 1992. The legislation requires states to pass and enforce laws that prohibit the sale of tobacco to individuals under 18 years of age. Since guidelines were put in place in 1996, states have consistently improved their compliance rates. In 2006 all states were in

> **In addition to addressing supply and demand, preventing teen smoking requires understanding why young people try cigarettes and the reasons that they become habitual smokers.**

compliance with rules that no more than 20 percent of retailers be cited for violating cigarette sales laws.

Despite these efforts, cigarettes and other tobacco products remain readily available to minors who want them. Today, over half of eighth graders and three-quarters of tenth graders say they could get cigarettes "fairly easily" or "very easily." In addition to stronger law enforcement, antitobacco organizations advocate more stringent laws, such as increasing the minimum age for cigarette sales and banning sales over the Internet or in vending machines.

For many years, Congress has considered legislation to increase the federal government's role in tobacco control. In 2009 President Barack Obama signed major antismoking legislation. The act gives the Food and Drug Administration oversight of tobacco products, a move that antismoking advocates believe will help to strengthen enforcement of existing laws and lessen the prevalence of smoking in the long run.

How Can Teen Smoking Be Prevented?

In addition to addressing supply and demand, preventing teen smoking requires understanding why young people try cigarettes and the reasons that they become habitual smokers. Antismoking organizations have engaged in comprehensive research into these issues. The Centers for Disease Control and Prevention (CDC) and the Substance Abuse and Mental Health Services Administration (SAMHSA) are among the government agencies that have invested millions of dollars in researching trends in tobacco use, including use among children and teens.

A host of nonprofit organizations also have spearheaded research projects and antismoking campaigns. These include national health organizations such as the American Lung Association and the American Cancer Society, as well as smaller organizations created specifically to prevent smoking among children and teens. These campaigns have proven to be most successful when they are combined with school- or community-based antismoking programs targeted at young people.

Research also indicates that reductions in smoking rates are linked to the perception of risk. Antismoking campaigns that convince young people of the serious health dangers of smoking cigarettes are most likely to have an impact. Parents, peers, and role models such as athletes or celebrities can play an important role in communicating this message.

How Serious a Problem Is Teen Smoking?

66Despite all the tobacco use on TV and in movies, music videos, billboards and magazines—most teens, adults, and athletes DON'T use tobacco.99

—Centers for Disease Control and Prevention, fact sheet, 2009.

66The fact that over a fifth of our young people are smoking when they leave high school, given all that is known today about the health consequences, is hardly the basis for complacency.99

—Lloyd D. Johnston, a senior researcher at the University of Michigan.

Roughly one in five American teens smokes cigarettes. While anti-smoking advocates argue that this rate is much too high, it is the lowest in decades. The *Monitoring the Future* study, for instance, shows a gradual increase in tobacco use in the early 1990s, peaking in the mid-1990s. Although the teen smoking rate has declined since then, the rate of decline has slowed in recent years. In 2008, 11.4 percent of high school seniors reported daily use of cigarettes, compared to 22.4 percent a decade prior.

Cigarettes contain over 4,000 chemicals, at least 63 of which have been proven to cause cancer. Lung cancer is perhaps the most obvious result of smoking, but tobacco use also causes cancers of the mouth, throat, esophagus, kidneys, stomach, and bladder. In addition to cancer, smoking cigarettes causes emphysema, a disease in which the tiny air sacs in the lungs are damaged, making it difficult for oxygen to pass from the lungs into the bloodstream. Some smokers also suffer from chronic bronchitis, an irritation and inflammation of the airways in the lungs.

Cigarette smoking has also been linked to heart disease. Nicotine causes blood vessels to squeeze together, resulting in an increase in blood pressure. This in turn increases the smoker's risk of a stroke or heart attack. The tar in cigarettes causes additional problems. The tar sticks to cilia, the little hairs in one's lungs that help keep them clean. This causes airways to swell and get clogged with mucus. This is the cause of "smoker's cough" and exacerbates asthmatic symptoms.

> " Lung cancer is perhaps the most obvious result of smoking, but tobacco use also causes cancers of the mouth, throat, esophagus, kidneys, stomach, and bladder. "

Smokers are also at higher risk of osteoporosis, a degenerative disease in which the bones become brittle and break easily. When children or teens smoke, it can retard lung growth and lung functioning. Research also shows that smoking can negatively impact sexual health and contribute to later fertility problems among both men and women.

Studies show that teens have higher rates of smoking during pregnancy than adults. In 2005, 16.6 percent of pregnant teens aged 15 to 19 smoked during pregnancy. The adverse effects of prenatal exposure to tobacco have been well documented. Scientists have used magnetic resonance imaging (MRI) scans to show that exposing an unborn fetus to tobacco can affect the brain all the way into early adulthood. Some researchers suggest that this may be one reason that children of smokers are more inclined to take up smoking themselves.

A 2009 study also showed a link between teen smoking and depression and other mental illnesses as an adult. "This study is unique because it is the first one to show that nicotine exposure early in life can have long-term neurobiological consequences evidenced in mood disorders," said Carlos Bolanos, one of the study's researchers. "In addition, the study indicates that even brief exposure to nicotine increases risk for mood disorders later in life."[5]

Other Consequences of Teen Smoking

While many health problems occur years after one begins smoking, some negative impacts are more immediate. Smoking restricts blood vessels, preventing oxygen and nutrients from nourishing the skin, which in turn increases the risk of psoriasis and other skin problems. Cigarettes also cause halitosis, a form of bad breath. Studies show that smokers are more susceptible than nonsmokers to colds, flu, bronchitis, pneumonia, and other illnesses. It also takes a smoker longer to get over an illness.

Tobacco use can negatively impact teens in a number of other ways. Smoking impairs athletic performance, for instance. Teens who smoke have less lung power, putting them at a disadvantage in sports activities. Some smokers—even as teens—become winded just from climbing a flight of stairs. Smoking also impedes the body's ability to produce collagen, which means that injuries to tendons and ligaments will heal more slowly.

Cigarette smoking also impacts sleep. A 2008 study showed that smokers spend more time in light or restless sleep than in deeper sleep. This can leave smokers more tired than nonsmokers even when they have been asleep for the same length of time. Scientists suspect that this is due to nicotine withdrawal that smokers experience because they are not smoking as they sleep.

For teens, poor sleep can translate to ongoing restlessness and tiredness during the day, negatively impacting school performance. Some experts suspect that this may contribute to the fact that teens who smoke tend to do less well in school than their nonsmoking peers. Experts disagree about why tobacco impacts school performance: Some say it is due to the fact smokers are in poor health and miss more school, while others suggest that young smokers may find it hard to concentrate with too much

> " Users of smokeless tobacco have a lower risk of developing lung cancer, but the many other health impacts of cigarette smoking apply to smokeless tobacco. "

nicotine in their systems or when going through nicotine withdrawal. Still others argue against causality: The fact that smokers do worse in school does not mean that this is due to the fact that they smoke.

Smoking, Drug Abuse, and Other High-Risk Behaviors

Tobacco use has also been associated with a range of other high-risk behaviors, including fighting, carrying weapons, and sexual promiscuity, as well as the use of alcohol, marijuana, and other illegal drugs. Health professionals warn that cigarettes might be a "gateway" to drug use. While a high percentage of people who use illegal drugs smoke cigarettes, some people argue that this does not mean that smoking leads to drug abuse. These researchers cite as proof that many adults smoke cigarettes and do not use illegal drugs or get into trouble with the law.

Depression, suicide attempts, and other mental health issues are more common in teen smokers than nonsmokers as well. Again, experts disagree about the reasons: Some experts say that it is depression that leads to smoking, not vice versa. Students may seek out smoking as a social tool to reduce their feelings of sadness. Unfortunately, this can lead to a vicious cycle. Teen smokers may face disapproval from teachers and peers, adding to their loneliness and insecurity.

How Bad Are Cloves, Bidis, Menthols, and Lights?

Many smokers recognize that serious health risks are associated with smoking, but they want to smoke anyway. Clove cigarettes, bidis, menthol cigarettes, and those labeled as light or low tar often appeal to teens who feel this way. In a 2007 report, the American Legacy Foundation reported that nearly 40 percent of youth smokers usually smoke light, ultra-light, or mild cigarettes; another 37 percent smoke menthol brands. A small, but growing number of teens also are smoking clove cigarettes and bidis.

People often choose these options because they believe them to be safer, but studies indicate otherwise. These cigarettes deliver the same amount of tar and nicotine—and thus health risks—as regular cigarettes. In fact, legislation passed in 2009 forbids tobacco companies from continuing to use "light" or other labels that imply these cigarettes are better for you than other types. The law also outlaws candy-flavored brands that legislators believe were designed to appeal to children and teens.

Menthol cigarettes are not included in the law even though some researchers claim that they may be more dangerous than regular cigarettes. "Mentholated smoke stimulates cold receptors in the lungs, causing the smoker to hold his or her breath longer when inhaling," explains a report of the American Legacy Foundation. Some experts worry that teens may turn to menthol brands as laws prohibit flavored tobacco products.

Dangers Associated with Cigars

Some teens believe that cigars have fewer health risks than cigarettes. Much of the reasoning centers around the fact that cigars are not inhaled as deeply. "I know cigarettes are bad for you, but what about cigars?" asks a teen blogger. "I don't inhale the smoke."[6]

According to health professionals, the answer is simple: Cigars are just as unhealthy as other tobacco products. The tobacco in cigars has the same negative health impacts as cigarettes and is just as addictive. The health risks increase with the number of cigars smoked and increase even more if cigar smoke is inhaled. Even when cigar smokers do not inhale the smoke directly, they are still exposed to the secondhand smoke. Furthermore, cigars are bigger and contain higher concentrations of tar and nicotine than cigarettes.

> While few people today would argue that cigarettes are good for you, many Americans believe that the health risks have been exaggerated.

It takes an hour or two on average to smoke a cigar—long enough for the harmful effects to take hold. "All tobacco products are toxic," warns TeenGrowth.com. "The notion that cigars are not as dangerous as cigarettes is a myth deliberately and elaborately promoted by the tobacco industry, as shown by internal memos from the Cigar Association of America."[7]

Is Smokeless Tobacco a Safe Alternative?

Many people believe that smokeless tobacco is safe—at least safer than cigarettes. Smokeless tobacco comes from the same tobacco plants as those rolled into cigarettes. Like cigarettes, the nicotine in smokeless tobacco is highly addictive. In fact, experts say that smokeless tobacco delivers a higher amount of nicotine than cigarettes or cigars. Chewing tobacco delivers about 4.6 milligrams of nicotine and snuff 3.6 milligrams, compared to 1.8 milligrams delivered by a cigarette.

> **The brain quickly gets used to nicotine; as tolerance increases, a higher dose is needed to get the same effect.**

Users of smokeless tobacco have a lower risk of developing lung cancer, but the many other health impacts of cigarette smoking apply to smokeless tobacco. The most serious problem is cancer of the mouth or larynx. Mouth cancer begins as leukoplakia, a white sore or plaque in the mouth that is typically found where the smokeless tobacco is held. Leukoplakia is present in the mouths of over 50 percent of the people who regularly chew tobacco or use snuff. According to the American Cancer Society, leukoplakia turns into cancer in 3 to 5 percent of cases.

Like cigarettes, smokeless tobacco also causes heart disease and high blood pressure. There are other health dangers associated with smokeless tobacco. About 25 percent of users experience receding gums. This leaves the roots of the teeth exposed to bacteria, which leaves a person at higher risk of tooth decay and bone loss.

Scott Marsee is among those who believed that smokeless tobacco was safer than cigarettes. Marsee began using smokeless tobacco at the age of 12 and soon became addicted. At 18, Marsee, a promising athlete, was diagnosed with cancer of the tongue. Part of his tongue was removed, but it was too late for Marsee: He died from cancer at the age of 19.

Are Health Risks Exaggerated?

While few people today would argue that cigarettes are good for you, some Americans believe that the health risks have been exaggerated. Rosalind Marimont, a mathematician at the National Institute of Health, and Robert Levy, a senior fellow at the Cato Institute, are among those who dispute the finding that more than 400,000 deaths in the United States are smoking related. Their analysis cited flaws in the methodology, including failing to control for diet, exercise, and other factors. According to these researchers, the smoking-related deaths had been overstated by more than 65 percent.

Some teens also believe that the media overstates the health risks. In the 2008 *Monitoring the Future* study, more than 20 percent of eighth graders said that the harmful effects of cigarettes have been exaggerated.

Dealing with Addiction

One of the main problems with teen smoking is that it quickly becomes addictive. The brain quickly gets used to nicotine; as tolerance increases, a higher dose is needed to get the same effect. Evidence also suggests that the younger people start smoking, the more quickly they become addicted. A 2007 study of sixth-grade smokers found that becoming addicted to nicotine can take just two days from when youths start inhaling cigarette smoke. Half of the children in the study were addicted by the time they were smoking just seven cigarettes a month.

Once addicted, it is very difficult to quit. The vast majority of teen smokers plan to quit, but only a handful will succeed. Eighty percent of adult smokers today started before they were 18. Health organizations offer a myriad of programs to help people quit smoking—from nicotine patches and gum to support groups and hypnotism. Clearly, the best way to reduce the number of smokers and the adverse health effects is to prevent people from ever starting. This requires figuring out why people smoke and who is to blame—an issue that has been at the center of the smoking controversy for many years.

How Serious a Problem Is Teen Smoking?

❝Smoking among the younger generation is more common than many people think.❞

—nottosmoke.com, "Adverse Effects of Smoking on Young People," 2009. www.nottosmoke.com.

Nottosmoke.com is an antismoking Web site providing facts for people who want to quit.

❝I can't begin to tell you what a dramatic difference [the decline in teen smoking] is going to make in the health and longevity of this generation.❞

—Lloyd D. Johnston, press release, December 11, 2008. www.monitoringthefuture.org.

Johnston is the principal investigator of the annual *Monitoring the Future* study.

"More progress must be made to ensure youngsters at critical age levels continue to turn away from smoking."

—Cheryl Healton, "Statement on the Centers for Disease Control's Report on Cigarette Smoking Among High School Students," June 17, 2009. www.prnewswire.com.

Healton is the president and CEO of the American Legacy Foundation.

"Tobacco captivates people when they cannot rationally resist its siren call and can unleash a slow, deadly disease that can kill them even as they try to escape the tenacious trap of addiction."

—Tim Johnson, "The Role of the Media in Promoting and Reducing Tobacco Use," June 2008.

Johnson, a physician, is medical editor of ABC News.

"Tobacco historically has been used as a medicine to treat a variety of conditions, and more recently, research has revealed an important connection to nicotine and increased brain function."

—Gary Manelski, "Health Benefits of Cigars," Gary's Cigars Blog, August 5, 2008. http://cigars.about.com.

Manelski is a cigar connoisseur and writer.

"Children and teens don't think much about future health outcomes."

—American Cancer Society, "Child and Teen Tobacco Use," October 3, 2008. www.cancer.org.

The American Cancer Society is a national organization committed to fighting cancer.

> **❝One belief that has proven to influence the likelihood that young people use a drug is their belief about whether its use poses a danger for the user. For cigarettes, there has been a substantial increase . . . in the proportions of teens who see pack-a-day smoking as involving great risk.❞**

—University of Michigan, "More Good News on Teen Smoking: Rates at or Near Record Lows," news release, December 11, 2008.

The University of Michigan has conducted annual *Monitoring the Future* surveys of high school students since 1991.

> **❝I always swore I would quit [smoking], and I really tried. But I started smoking at 11 or 12 years old. . . . [Today] I'm sick, I'm tired, I'm in pain all the time, and I have cancer and emphysema. It has drained my energy, my health, and my opportunity to do things with my kids.❞**

—Deborah Scott, "I'm Deborah and Smoking Has Smoked This Body," whyquit.com, September 2007. http://whyquit.com.

Scott was diagnosed with cancer at 38 years old. She has already lost both her parents to cigarette smoking.

How Serious a Problem Is Teen Smoking?

- The American Lung Association estimates that every minute, about **4,800 teens** take a first drag of a cigarette; about **2,000** of them will go on to become chain smokers.

- More than **3.5 million** U.S. high school students—roughly **20 percent** of the total—smoke cigarettes.

- Research shows that **87 percent** of students who smoke one cigarette or more a day are physically dependent on nicotine.

- According to the CDC, if current tobacco use patterns persist, an estimated **6.4 million** current smokers under 18 will eventually die prematurely from a smoking-related disease.

- Among racial and ethnic subgroups, approximately **23 percent** of white, **17 percent** of Hispanic, and **12 percent** of African American high school students smoked cigarettes in 2007.

- According to the *Monitoring the Future* survey, the rates of teen smoking increased gradually during the early 1990s and peaked at **36.4 percent** in 1997.

- The rate of teen tobacco use in 2008 was at its lowest level ever; the percentage of eighth graders who ever smoked a cigarette was down from **49 percent** in 1996 to **21 percent** in 2008.

Teens and Tobacco Use

This chart shows the percentage of teens, aged 12 to 17, who reported that they had used different tobacco products during a 1-month period. While overall tobacco use decreased between 2002 and 2007, use of smokeless tobacco increased slightly. Cigarettes remain the most widely used tobacco product among teens; more than twice as many teens smoke cigarettes than cigars.

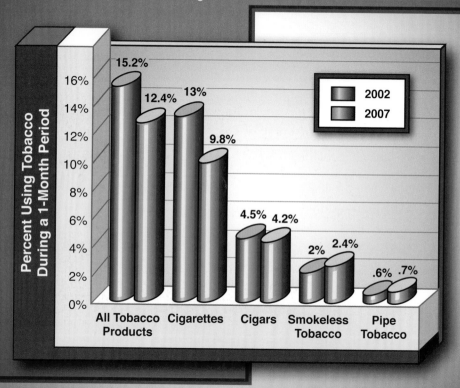

Source: Substance Abuse and Mental Health Services Administration, "Results from the 2007 National Survey on Drug Use and Health: National Findings," September 2008. http://oas.samhsa.gov.

- The CDC estimates that smokers cost the country **$96 billion** a year in direct health care costs, and an additional **$97 billion** a year in lost productivity.

- Cigarettes contain over **4,000 chemicals**, at least **63** of which have been proven to cause cancer.

Teen Smoking Rates Are Declining

Smoking rates among eighth, tenth, and twelfth graders are at their lowest levels since the *Monitoring the Future* survey began (in 1975 for twelfth graders and in 1991 for eighth and tenth graders). Experts believe that the changes brought about by the 1998 Master Settlement Agreement with the tobacco industry have played a part in the decline since the mid-1990s. This graph shows the number of students who have smoked one or more cigarettes during a recent 30-day period. With smoking rates for high school seniors above 20 percent, anti-smoking advocates say there is still a lot of progress to be made.

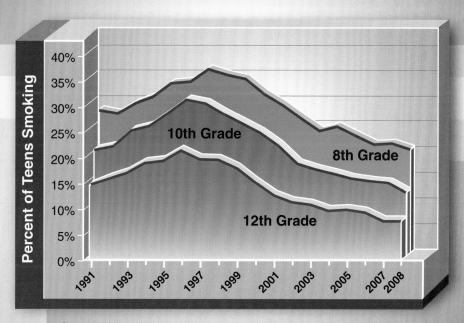

Source: University of Michigan, *Monitoring the Future National Results on Adolescent Drug Use: Overview of Key Findings, 2008.* Bethesda, MD: National Institute on Drug Abuse, 2009.

- Cigarette smoking alone accounts for **30 percent** of all cancer cases and over **85 percent** of lung cancer cases.

- According to the CDC, on average, adults who smoke die **14 years** earlier than nonsmokers. Each cigarette takes **5 to 20 minutes** off a smoker's life.

White Teens Smoke More than African American and Hispanic Teens

Smoking rates are consistently higher for white teens than for African American teens. Some experts speculate that this may be due to cultural differences, including parents' rules about and attitudes toward smoking as well the attitudes of peers. Antismoking advocates say that the lower levels among some groups of teens is proof that lower rates of teen smoking can be achieved. For all races, the percentage of teen boys who smoke is higher than the percentage for girls, but the difference is less significant for whites than for African Americans or Hispanics.

Percentage of high school students who reported in 2007 that they had smoked one or more cigarettes in the past 30 days.

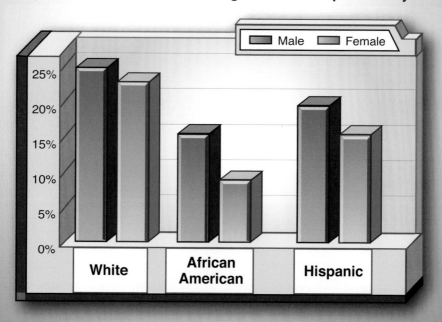

Source: U.S. Centers for Disease Control and Prevention, Youth Risk Behavior Survey, 2001–2007 in "Cigarette Use Among High School Students—United States, 1991–2007," *Morbidity and Mortality Weekly Report*, June 6, 2008.

- Teen smokers are 3 times more likely to use alcohol, 8 times more likely to smoke marijuana, and **22 times** more likely to use cocaine than their nonsmoking peers.

Who Is to Blame for Teen Smoking?

66Manufacturers have become more aggressive in targeting high-risk groups, including minorities and youth, with aggressive advertising, redesigned products with more nicotine, introducing candy-like flavored products, and aggressively marketing brands popular with young African-Americans.99

—Gregory N. Connolly, professor of the practice of public health at Harvard University School of Public Health.

66There would be far fewer teen smokers in America today if state spending on tobacco control followed levels recommended by the federal Centers for Disease Control and Prevention.99

—Chuck Alexander, spokesperson at impacTEEN.

A number of interrelated factors influence whether teens choose to smoke. As with any other decision, deciding whether to smoke often is influenced by circumstances, including whether those around a teen are smoking. The decision is also influenced by the consequences of the action—or more importantly the teen's perception of the consequences. Teens' perceptions may be influenced by friends and peers, parents and other family members, athletes and celebrities, television and movies, and cigarette advertising and promotions. The American Cancer Society warns: "Children and teens are easy targets for the tobacco industry. They're often influenced by TV, movies, advertising, and by what their friends do and say. They don't realize what a struggle it can be to quit, and having cancer, emphysema, blindness, or impotence may not seem like real concerns."[8]

Peer Pressure

During adolescence people pull away from parents and authority figures and look to peers for guidance about attitudes and behaviors. During these years peer pressure can be hard to ignore. In fact, peer pressure is one of the most common reasons that youths say they start smoking.

In some cases best friends or a small clique of teens join together to try their first cigarette; later, smoking may become a bonding experience. A friend who does not smoke may feel left out and begin smoking to fit in. Studies have revealed that the rate of smoking among young people with three or more friends who smoke is 10 times greater than the rate among young people whose friends do not smoke.

> **In some cases, smoking is one of the only things that a group of teens has in common; as time goes on, the ritual of smoking may serve as the glue that holds such groups together.**

In addition, teens may choose to smoke to portray themselves as "tough" or "cool." This can be a particularly compelling reason for students who are teased or are insecure. Other teens—perhaps those who are "outsiders" who do not fit in with the main groups at school— may start smoking to fit in with a group of smokers. In some cases smoking is one of the only things that a group of teens has in common; as time goes on, the ritual of smoking may serve as the glue that holds such groups together.

Parental Influence

The attitudes and behavior of parents may also influence attitudes about smoking. Parents serve as important role models when children are young and forming opinions about right and wrong behaviors. Some children who see their parents smoke from a very young age may decide that this is a normal or natural behavior. Even when parents say that smoking is unhealthy, a child's desire to emulate adult behavior sometimes overrides health concerns.

The research about the impact of parental smoking is inconclusive, however. Some studies suggest that the correlation between parental smoking and teen smoking may be rooted in genetics. Other studies suggest that parental smoking does not influence the attitudes of children toward smoking. Many children of smokers never take up the habit. In fact, kids are often the primary motivators who encourage parents to quit.

> 66 **Cigarette companies have consistently denied targeting youth, but critics say Joe Camel provides strong evidence to the contrary.** 99

Regardless, experts warn parents not to look the other way if they suspect (or know) that their child is smoking. "We've talked to teens who say, 'If my mom and dad really cared, they'd push me on it,'"[9] says Lyndon Haviland, the executive vice president of the American Legacy Foundation. Haley, a 16-year-old smoker, agrees: "I think if I was grounded every time I got caught smoking or if my phone got taken away, then it would definitely make it harder to keep smoking."[10] Researchers speculate that one reason teen smoking rates may be lower in Hispanic households is because Hispanic parents are less likely to allow teens to smoke in the house, even when the parents themselves smoke.

The Role of Tobacco Marketing

A primary goal of marketing is to attract new consumers. Opponents of tobacco marketing say this is imperative for tobacco companies, who need to replace the hundreds of thousands of smokers who have died from tobacco use, as well as those who have succeeded in quitting. Critics of the tobacco industry say that cigarette companies focus many of their campaigns on young people, not only to get them to start smoking but also because they tend to have strong brand loyalty.

Cigarette companies have consistently denied targeting youth with these messages, but critics say Joe Camel provides strong evidence to the contrary. Between 1987 and 1997 Joe Camel, a cartoon mascot for R.J.

Reynolds's Camel brand cigarettes, was shown in advertisements smoking cigarettes in all types of situations. In a study funded by R.J. Reynolds Tobacco Company in the mid-1990s, 72 percent of 6-year-olds and 52 percent of children aged 3–6 years could identify Joe Camel, and 95 percent of these children knew that he sold cigarettes.

> **Cigarettes remain one of the most heavily marketed products in the United States. The tobacco industry spends billions of dollars each year on cigarette advertising and promotion.**

Internal documents revealed during lawsuits in the 1990s also showed that tobacco companies wanted to attract young consumers. "The base of our business is the high school student,"[11] advised an executive at Lorillard Tobacco in a memo. A 1981 Philip Morris memo states, "Today's teenager is tomorrow's potential regular customer, and the overwhelming majority of smokers first begin to smoke while still in their teens. . . . The smoking patterns of teenagers are particularly important to Philip Morris."[12] In the first decade of the twenty-first century, Philip Morris spent over $100 million per year to advertise Marlboro, the top-selling brand among underage smokers.

The purpose of advertisements for any product is to influence consumer behavior. For tobacco companies, this means taking up smoking. To accomplish this goal, cigarette advertisements consistently portray smokers as being suave, rugged, or sexy. Some early advertisements also boasted the health benefits of smoking. The Marlboro Man was a lasting example of a successful icon selling a brand.

Changes in Tobacco Marketing

The 1998 Master Settlement Agreement (MSA) forced tobacco companies to change their marketing strategies. The MSA specifically prohibits marketing tobacco products to children and teens and outlaws cartoon characters like Joe Camel. Since the MSA, within just three years, tobacco companies had increased marketing expenditures by two-thirds.

Today, cigarettes remain one of the most heavily marketed products in the United States. The tobacco industry spends billions of dollars each year on cigarette advertising and promotion.

Tobacco companies once devoted 20 percent of their marketing budgets to magazine advertisements, but these ads now consist of less than 1 percent of total marketing expenses. The largest percentage of marketing dollars goes to price discounts paid to retailers or wholesalers in order to reduce the cost of cigarettes for consumers. Tobacco companies also have increased expenditures in point-of-purchase displays at convenience stores and gas stations. Some of these displays are placed in store windows or along busy roads, reinforcing brand messages each day to thousands of people passing by—including children and teens.

Tobacco companies also compete for new smokers by offering discounted prices on cigarette brands most often smoked by adolescents; developing products (such as hats or T-shirts) with brands or logos; and sponsoring concerts, sports competitions, and other events. For many years tobacco companies and their brands gained visibility through sponsorships of U.S. auto racing teams, for instance, splashing their product names across the hoods of their NASCAR and Formula One automobiles and on the clothing and gear of drivers and pit crews. Following the U.S. ban on TV advertising in the 1970s, R.J. Reynolds sponsored the NASCAR Championship; the "Winston Cup" proved to be a highly effective way to advertise its brand to millions of TV viewers. Similarly, for several decades Virginia Slims sponsored an annual women's professional tennis championship as part of the campaign to attract women smokers.

How Tobacco Companies Restrict Youth Access

Tobacco companies sponsor a number of programs intended to reduce teen access. The Coalition for Responsible Tobacco Retailing, which includes the major U.S. tobacco manufacturers as well as retail and wholesale associations, sponsors the "We Card" program. The program offers a range of tools and resources to help prevent underage tobacco sales, including training seminars, interactive online training, in-store signage and educational resources, including tip sheets on how to spot fake IDs.

In addition, some tobacco companies provide retailers with "We Card" signage and signs reminding adults not to buy products for minors. Some companies also offer incentives to retailers who merchandise and sell cigarettes in ways that support youth access prevention efforts. Philip Morris, for instance, "imposes penalties on stores that are fined, cited, or convicted of illegal tobacco product sales to underage purchasers."[13]

The Influence of Movies

For many years antismoking advocates have warned that tobacco use in movies encourages young people to smoke. Studies have shown that teens are more likely to try smoking following exposure to smoking in the movies and/or television. A 2003 study by researchers at Dartmouth College, for instance, concluded that smoking in movies is the most powerful pro-tobacco influence on kids today, accounting for 52 percent of adolescents who start smoking, an effect even stronger than cigarette advertising. Research also suggests that teens who see a lot of smoking in movies have more favorable attitudes toward smoking and characters who smoke.

The prevalence of smoking in movies is alarming to antismoking advocates. In a 2008 report, the U.S. National Cancer Institute found that more than three-quarters of box-office hit movies showed cigarette smoking and that identifiable cigarette brands appear in about one-third of these movies. Like earlier studies, the report concluded that young people who were exposed to smoking in movies were far more likely to try cigarettes than those who were not.

> **Studies have shown that young people are more likely to try smoking following exposure to smoking in the movies and/or television.**

Smoking is not restricted to movies for adults; smoking is common also in movies with "PG-13" and "G" ratings, presumably created for and targeted at children. The latest research shows that PG-13 films account for two of every three tobacco impressions delivered to audiences of all ages. Children's movies such as *101 Dalmations* (and the sequel), *George of the Jungle*, *The Incredibles*, and *Muppets from Space* have all included smoking scenes.

Research suggests that seeing smoking at the movies can influence even very young children to smoke later in life. "Media effects are complex and multidimensional," concludes the National Cancer Institute, "Media can have short-term effects such as the impact of a short burst of advertising on consumer attitudes and behaviors—for example, on sales of cigarettes—and long-term effects that are stable and sustaining, such as on social norms and values."[14]

The motion picture industry says that the amount of smoking in movies is overstated. "In our regular dialogue with parents, they frequently note that depictions of smoking in films have significantly declined in recent years," says a spokesperson. "They often tell us that they cannot recall a recent incident in which they took their child to a G, PG, or PG-13 film and found a scene involving smoking that was objectionable."[15]

Spreading Blame for Movie Images

Some people blame the tobacco industry for the amount of smoking in movies. "Big tobacco companies know the power of movies," concludes the fact sheet at the Smoke Free Movies Web site. "Moving stories with charismatic actors are a powerful way to attract new smokers and keep current smokers."[16]

Critics also are troubled by the fact that brands popular among teens are those that are most often shown in movies. Marlboro, the most popular brand of cigarettes among young people, is depicted in movies far more than any other brand.

The tobacco industry denies any wrongdoing. Philip Morris proclaims that its policy "since 1990 has been both to refrain from paying for product placement and to decline all third-party requests to use, display or reference our cigarette brands, products, packages or advertisements in any movies or television shows or other public entertainment media."[17]

Antismoking advocates blame movie executives as well as the tobacco industry. "We believe that producers, directors and others involved in the creative process are in a unique position to voluntarily eliminate smoking scenes in movies and other public entertainment media directed at youth," says a Philip Morris spokesperson.[18] The American Medical Association is among the organizations that have called for a ban on smoking in "G" and "PG" films. In 2007 the Motion Picture Association of America began including smoking as one of the factors to be considered in a film's rating.

Factors Influencing Teen Decisions

When looking for the reasons that young people continue to smoke despite the obvious health consequences, the tobacco industry is an easy scapegoat, particularly since internal documents have come to light that show that they have lied to the public in the past. Still, a lot more is involved in the decision to smoke than advertising. Smoking remains part of American life. Evidence suggests that the more teens see people smoking, the more apt they are to take up the habit themselves. But even teens who are relatively sheltered from the influence of smokers sometimes try cigarettes. They may want to fit in with friends. They may see smoking as a way to rebel. They may just be curious. Addressing teen smoking requires recognizing that smoking is a choice and understanding the reasons why teens make this choice.

Who Is to Blame for Teen Smoking?

66 **Young teens are influenced profoundly by celebrity behavior, and they will do whatever it takes to be cool.** 99

—Common Sense Media, "Smoking in the Media Tips," May 19, 2009.www.commonsensemedia.org.

Common Sense Media is a nonprofit organization that monitors media and entertainment affecting young people and families.

....

66 **Teens are more likely to start smoking if parents or close peers/family do. Not just because some celebrity does.** 99

—Fourteen-year-old Rhode Island teen contributor, "Smoking in the Media Tips," Common Sense Media, May 19, 2009.
www.commonsensemedia.org.

This 14-year-old from Rhode Island was responding to commentary on the connection between teen smoking and celebrities.

....

Bracketed quotes indicate conflicting positions.

* Editor's Note: While the definition of a primary source can be narrowly or broadly defined, for the purposes of Compact Research, a primary source consists of: 1) results of original research presented by an organization or researcher; 2) eyewitness accounts of events, personal experience, or work experience; 3) first-person editorials offering pundits' opinions; 4) government officials presenting political plans and/or policies; 5) representatives of organizations presenting testimony or policy.

❝ Peer pressure is the number-one reason young people start to smoke. ❞

—J. Poolos, "Tobacco and Nicotine," *Teen Health and Wellness: Real Life, Real Answers*, March 2009. www.teenhealthandwellness.com.

Poolos is the author of several children's books and writes on a variety of issues for young people.

❝ Sometimes teen smoking is a form of rebellion or a way to fit in with a particular group of friends. Some teens light up in an attempt to lose weight or to feel better about themselves. Others smoke to feel cool or independent. ❞

—Mayo Clinic, "Teen Smoking: 10 Ways to Help Teens Stay Smoke-Free," Tween and Teen Health, June 17, 2009.

The Mayo Clinic is a highly respected not-for-profit medical practice dedicated to the diagnosis, treatment, and prevention of illness.

❝ Smoking can be a family habit. Researchers say teens are more likely to smoke if they see a parent do it. ❞

—Ira Dreyfuss, "Smoking and Parents' Examples," *HHS Healthbeat*, February 18, 2009. www.hhs.gov.

Dreyfuss is a public affairs specialist at the U.S. Department of Health and Human Services.

❝ If your child wants to [smoke], at some point, they will come to the age that they really do not care about what you tell them to do. They do not care if you [disapprove], so do not bother. ❞

—Parent, "Smoking, Drinking, and Peer Pressure," Parents.com, May 14, 2008. www.parents.com.

This parent wrote in response to an article on talking to kids about the dangers of smoking.

&&Much tobacco advertising targets the psychological needs of adolescents, such as popularity, peer acceptance, and positive self-image. Advertising creates the perception that smoking will satisfy these needs.

—National Cancer Institute, "The Role of the Media in Promoting and Reducing Tobacco Use," Tobacco Control Monograph 19, June 2008, p. 290.

The National Cancer Institute is the U.S. government's principal agency for cancer research.

&&Having involved parents—those who know a lot about their children's friends, activities, and how they're doing in school—can help children overcome peer influence to start smoking.

—Emily Halevy, "Smoking Addiction," Connect with Kids, August 15, 2007. www.connectwithkids.com.

Halevy is a producer at Connect with Kids.

&&Unfortunately, the big-screen appeal of smoking movie stars and other celebrities is a strong influence for young people to start smoking.

—David Kaufman, "Smoking on Screen and on the Field: Athletes and Celebs Who Smoke," March 21, 2008. www.healthcentral.com.

Kaufman is a physician who writes about the dangers of tobacco use and the importance of quitting.

&&As a smoker I can't remember the last time I watched a Hollywood film and got an urge to smoke.

—Smokeen.com, "Reports Say That Movies and Advertising Main Cause for Teen Smoking," May 4, 2009.

Smokeen.com is a Web site that expresses the views of smokers and others who feel that smoking is their right.

66 Any film that shows or implies tobacco [use] should be rated 'R.' The only exceptions should be when the presentation of tobacco clearly and unambiguously reflects the dangers and consequences of tobacco use or is necessary to represent the smoking of a real historical figure.99

—AMA Alliance Screen Out! "The 4 Solutions," 2007. www.screenout.org.

The American Medical Association (AMA) Alliance has joined with national health groups to advocate for youth-rated films to be free of tobacco and its associated images.

66 Some have called for a 'mandatory R' rating on all films that contain any smoking. We do not believe such a step would further the specific goal of providing information to parents on this issue.99

—Dan Glickman, "Film Rating Board to Consider Smoking as a Factor," Motion Picture Association of America, press release, May 10, 2007. www.mpaa.org.

Glickman is the chairman and CEO of the Motion Picture Association of America.

Who Is to Blame for Teen Smoking?

- The smoking rate among kids who have three or more friends who smoke is **10 times higher** than the rate among kids who report that none of their friends smoke.

- An 11-year study found that **99 percent** of regular young smokers lived with at least one smoker. Less than **15 percent** said they had ever felt under pressure to take up cigarettes.

- One 2007 study showed that **73 percent** of 11- to 17-year-olds who smoked cigarettes were with 1 or more friends when they tried their first cigarette, and **65 percent** of them got their first cigarette from a friend's pack.

- Kids whose parents smoke are more than **twice as likely** to smoke as kids whose parents do not smoke.

- Young children may be more susceptible to parent smoking than teens. In one study children who were under 13 when their parents were actively smoking were about **3.6 times** as likely to smoke as children of nonsmokers, while those who were 13 or older were about **1.7 times** more likely to use tobacco.

- The U.S. tobacco industry spent roughly **$15.3 billion** on tobacco marketing and promotion in 2008. This amounts to **$41 million each day**.

Most Teen Smokers Have Friends Who Smoke

Many teens try their first cigarette with a friend and continue to smoke because their friends do. As this chart shows, almost 50 percent of teen smokers say that all or most of their friends smoke, less than 1 percent of teen smokers have friends who do not smoke.

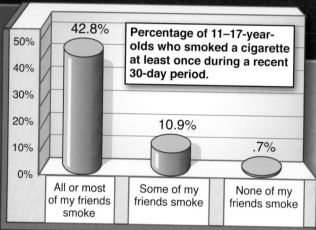

Percentage of 11–17-year-olds who smoked a cigarette at least once during a recent 30-day period.

- All or most of my friends smoke: 42.8%
- Some of my friends smoke: 10.9%
- None of my friends smoke: .7%

Teen Smoking Is More Likely If One or More Parents Smoke

Studies routinely show that teens are more likely to take up smoking if one or both parents smoke. This 2008 study by Philip Morris shows that kids whose parents smoke are more than twice as likely to smoke as kids whose parents do not smoke. Other studies show that a parent's smoking can impact the decision to smoke even if the child is very young when the parent smokes.

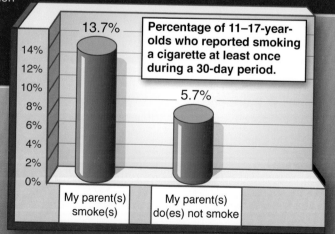

Percentage of 11–17-year-olds who reported smoking a cigarette at least once during a 30-day period.

- My parent(s) smoke(s): 13.7%
- My parent(s) do(es) not smoke: 5.7%

Source: Philip Morris USA Youth Smoking Prevention, "Peer Pressure & Smoking," brochure, 2008.

Tobacco Companies Tempt Teens with Flavored Cigarettes

Antismoking advocates accuse the tobacco companies of continuing to target teens, citing the introduction of candy- and fruit-flavored cigarettes as an example. The American Legacy Foundation studied the brands and types of cigarettes that teens preferred and found that most teens thought that a flavored cigarette would taste better than a regular cigarette. Critics of the tobacco industry also claim that the evidence shows that cigarette companies are trying to find products to attract African American and Hispanic teens, who have lower rates of smoking than white teens.

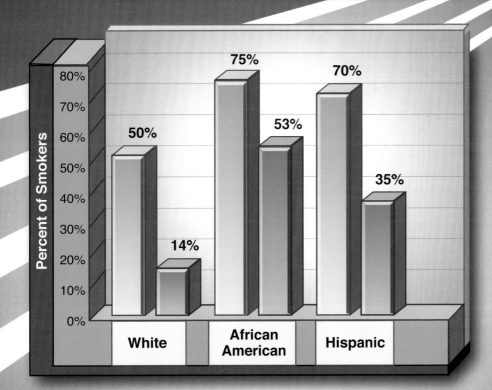

Percent of youth smokers who had heard of flavored cigarettes and thought that a flavored cigarette would taste better than a regular cigarette.

Percent of youth smokers who had tried flavored cigarettes

Source: American Legacy Foundation, "Cigarette Preferences Among Youth," *First Look Report*, June 2007.

Many Movies Show Tobacco Use

Many antismoking advocates believe that Hollywood is partly to blame for the large number of youths who smoke. The American Legacy Foundation studied the incidences of tobacco use or imagery in top box-office movies. According to their findings, the percentage of movies that include smoking characters has declined, but over half of the movies in 2005—even those rated G or PG—still had characters that smoke.

Percent of Movies with Tobacco Imagery, by Year of Release and Rating

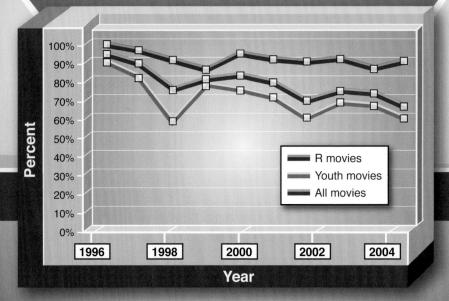

Source: American Legacy Foundation, "Characters Smoking in Top Box Office Movies," *First Look Report*, October 2007.

- A 2008 survey showed that kids are almost twice as likely as adults to recall tobacco advertising. Only **24 percent** of adults recalled seeing a tobacco ad in the 2 weeks prior to the survey; **47 percent** of teens 12–17 reported that they had seen such ads.

- Cigarette smoking is depicted in over **75 percent** of contemporary box-office hits. Identifiable cigarette brands appear in about one-third of movies. Leading actors light up in **60 percent** of movies.

- Tobacco use is found in about **20 percent** of television shows and **25 percent** of music videos.

- A 2007 report of the Institute of Medicine found that adolescents with higher exposure to smoking in movies are **2 to 2.7 times more likely** to try cigarette smoking in the future.

- Nonsmoking teens whose favorite stars frequently smoke on screen are **16 times more likely** to have positive attitudes about smoking in the future.

How Should Teen Smoking Be Regulated?

❝Public officials know precisely how to win this war [on smoking]—by raising taxes to make cigarettes too expensive for teens, funding creative anti-smoking campaigns and banning smoking in public places.❞

—*USA Today* editorial board.

❝The nation has made significant progress in reducing smoking among both youth and adults over the last 10 years, but that progress has slowed in recent years and further progress is at risk without aggressive efforts at all levels of government.❞

—Eric Lindblom, director for policy research and general counsel for the Campaign for Tobacco-Free Kids.

Few tobacco regulations existed in the United States until the 1960s, after the surgeon general issued the first warning about the dangers of smoking. Early laws focused on the ways in which tobacco products could be marketed. Congress banned cigarette advertisements on television and radio in 1969. In the 1998 Master Settlement Agreement (MSA) the tobacco companies agreed to refrain from targeting children and youth in their advertisements and promotions.

Congress has considered more stringent antismoking and tobacco control legislation for decades, but garnering the support needed to

52

pass comprehensive legislation has proven difficult. In 2009 President Obama, admitting that he himself began smoking as a teen, signed the most comprehensive tobacco bill in history. The Family Smoking Prevention and Tobacco Control Act of 2009 gives cigarette production and marketing oversight to the Food and Drug Administration (FDA), which many people believe will result in stricter enforcement of tobacco control laws.

The Debate over Minimum Age

Setting and enforcing laws pertaining to the minimum age for tobacco sales remains under the purview of the states. In all 50 states and the District of Columbia, selling tobacco products to minors is illegal. In 1991 Alabama became the first state to raise the minimum age to 19; as of 2009 Alaska, Utah, and New Jersey, as well as several local governments, have followed Alabama's example. In recent years, some antismoking advocates have called for increasing the age to 21.

Antismoking advocates believe that a higher minimum age would prevent young teens from smoking because students in younger grades in high school could no longer get cigarettes from seniors who just turned 18. Jessica Adelson, a 17-year-old Connecticut student, used this argument when suggesting legislation to raise the age to 21. "By increasing the age, we can stop many young people from getting their hands on cigarettes," Adelson testified at a hearing of the Connecticut General Assembly's Public Health Committee. "Why are we allowing our youth of Connecticut to start such a nasty habit at such a young and vulnerable age?"[19]

> " In 2009 President Obama, admitting that he himself began smoking as a teen, signed the the Family Smoking Prevention and Tobacco Control Act, the most comprehensive tobacco bill in history. "

Not everyone agrees that changing the minimum age would reduce teen smoking, however. Research suggests that most teen smokers—even as young as 14 or 15—purchase their own cigarettes despite the laws.

Many antismoking advocates say the focus should not be on raising the minimum age but on more stringent enforcement of current laws.

Enforcement of Cigarette Sales Laws

Tobacco sales are regulated by state governments. To address illegal sales of tobacco to minors, Congress enacted the Synar Amendment as part of the Alcohol, Drug Abuse, and Mental Health Reorganization Act of 1992.

The Synar Amendment requires all states to have a law prohibiting sales of tobacco products to minors and to enforce such laws "in a manner that can reasonably be expected to reduce the extent to which tobacco products are available to individuals under the age of 18."[20] The law also requires annual random, unannounced inspections of stores that sell tobacco products to ensure compliance. It called on states to develop a strategy that would achieve an inspection failure rate of less than 20 percent. States that did not comply with these provisions would lose federal funding for substance abuse and treatment programs.

The most common way to enforce laws prohibiting cigarette sales to minors is through the use of underage decoys. Essentially, this involves hiring teens under the age of 18 to try to purchase tobacco at convenience stores and other outlets. In controlled studies, communities with strong enforcement of tobacco control laws have seen lower rates of teen smoking than those that are more lax.

Wide differences in tobacco control among states remain. For instance, some states depend on law enforcement agencies while others govern tobacco control through departments of health or alcohol and tobacco control boards.

Other Tobacco Control Measures

In addition to prohibiting the sale of tobacco products to minors, some states have enacted other laws to make it harder for youth to buy cigarettes. For instance, requiring tobacco products to be placed behind the counter can discourage sales to minors because many teens are reluctant to ask the cashier for cigarettes. This also prevents shoplifting by underage teens and decreases impulse purchases.

Cigarette vending machines are illegal in several states. Where they are allowed, many states confine vending machines to bars, private clubs, casinos, and other adult-only facilities. Laws require identification for purchasing cigarettes from a vending machine. In most places the purchaser must show an ID to a bartender or cashier, who then turns on the cigarette machine with the push of a button. In Japan, where the minimum age for buying cigarettes is 20, new machines are equipped with technology that can detect a person's age.

> " Research suggests that most teen smokers—even as young as 14 or 15—purchase their own cigarettes despite the laws. "

Antismoking advocates say that self-service machines make it easier for young people to purchase cigarettes, but the vending machine industry points out that the vast majority of teens say they purchase their cigarettes from retailers and that establishments with vending machines require identification. Nationwide, the number of cigarette vending machines peaked at about 700,000 in 1986; in 2007 only about 60,000 machines were still in use.

Internet sales are another concern. Many online vendors simply require consumers to type in their birth date or click a box confirming that they are 18 years or older. One recent study found that only 6.3 percent of Internet vendors requested photo identification for tobacco purchases. A few states require Internet retailers to see valid identification when the sale is made electronically *and* upon delivery, but most states say such laws are impractical. In a 2007 report the Institute of Medicine concluded that "the only practical way to effectively regulate online tobacco retailers is through legislation prohibiting both online tobacco sales and shipment of tobacco products directly to consumers."[21]

The Master Settlement Agreement of 1998

In the mid-1990s several states sued tobacco companies to recover state-funded medical costs for treating smokers. The tobacco companies settled several lawsuits with individual states (Mississippi, Florida, Texas, and Minnesota) before signing the Master Settlement Agreement (MSA) with the remaining 46 states, the District of Columbia, and the 5 U.S. territories in 1998. The states also signed a similar agreement with United States Tobacco, the leading smokeless tobacco company.

Reducing youth smoking was a specific aim of the MSA. The MSA bans the direct or indirect targeting of minors in tobacco advertising, marketing, and promotions. The MSA also prohibits tobacco companies from using cartoon characters, such as the highly successful "Joe Camel" campaign; advertising on billboards; paying for product placement in media; and giving out free samples (except in adults-only facilities).

Studies suggest that the MSA has had little impact on the rates of tobacco use among adults but find some indication that it has contributed to a decline in the smoking rate among children and teens. The changes are due not only to the restrictions on advertising but also because tobacco companies had to raise the price of cigarettes to recoup the costs of the settlement. Research shows that teens are particularly sensitive to increases in tobacco prices, and researchers believe this may have been a major factor in the decline in teen smoking rates in the early 2000s.

The Family Prevention and Tobacco Control Act of 2009

In June 2009, President Obama signed major antitobacco legislation. The Family Smoking Prevention and Tobacco Control Act makes it illegal to sell candy- or fruit-flavored cigarettes, which lawmakers contended were particularly attractive to children and teens. The legislation also strengthened restrictions on tobacco marketing and advertising. It outlaws tobacco ads within 1,000 feet of schools and playgrounds and prohibits tobacco companies from using their logos for sports or entertainment events or placing logos on athletic wear and other items.

> " Many antismoking advocates say the focus should not be on raising the minimum age but on more stringent enforcement of current laws. "

Other provisions of the new bill are intended to increase the message about the dangers of smoking. In light of research showing that smokers assume that "light" or "mild" cigarettes are safer to smoke, the law also prohibits the use of these terms. The law gives oversight of tobacco products to the Food and Drug Administration (FDA). Analysts expect the FDA to require tobacco companies to list on their packaging the ingredients in their products and increase the size of warning labels. The FDA also plans to investigate claims that manufacturers have increased the amount of nicotine in tobacco products. Giving the FDA control over cigarettes and other tobacco products is highly controversial. In a 2009 Gallup poll, 52 percent of Americans—and 69 percent of smokers—said they disapproved of this action.

School Regulations

A few decades ago, many high schools had designated places for students to smoke. Today, almost all schools prohibit the use of tobacco on the premises at any time. Most high schools also prohibit tobacco at school events, including sports games, dances, and the like. Some schools have harsh punishments for students caught disobeying the smoking rules, including demerits or even suspension from school. School administrators hope to discourage smoking by making violations a permanent part of a student's record.

Advocates of strong smoking policies say that nonsmokers at schools in which others are seen smoking (even if it is not allowed) have a higher risk of starting to smoke themselves. A report by the American Cancer Society concluded there were several reasons for this: "As the prevalence of smoking among older students at a school increases, the chance of developing friendships with an older smoker may increase, smoking may seem more normative and acceptable, more social sources of cigarettes might exist, and it may seem that social prestige or popularity could be improved by smoking. These factors could make a younger student more apt to try smoking."[22]

> **In controlled studies, communities with strong enforcement of tobacco control laws have seen lower rates of teen smoking than those that are more lax.**

Not everyone agrees that strict rules are the best way to prevent smoking, however. Experts say some students see antismoking rules as a challenge. Many teens need to rebel and may enjoy the rush of smoking without getting caught.

> **The MSA bans the direct or indirect targeting of minors in tobacco advertising, marketing, and promotions.**

Other concerns center on punishments. Some people believe that disciplinary action should be reserved for more serious offenses and that students over 18 should not be punished for something that is legal. Parents may worry that it might be harder for their child to get into college if they have a violation on their record. Others say that a solution focused on punishment fails to address the real problem—addiction. One advocate for linking school rules to treatment writes, "Sadly, it is rare when any educator has an understanding of nicotine dependency or the principles necessary to recover from it."[23]

Should Smoking Be Banned in Public?

As of January 2009, 30 states, the District of Columbia, and hundreds of local governments had enacted smoke-free laws regulating smoking in bars, restaurants, and other public places. Some localities have expanded smoking bans to public parks, beaches, and other outdoor areas and prohibit smoking in a car when children are passengers.

Support for smoking bans is due largely to the dangers of secondhand smoke, which is shown to have negative effects for people who breathe it. Smoking bans also help reduce teen smoking rates because they limit exposure to adults modeling smoking behaviors and thus can help reduce the risk of teens starting to smoke.

Some smokers worry that smoking will be outlawed altogether. Some people believe that the dangers of secondhand smoke have been overestimated—that many illnesses attributed to secondhand smoke in fact have other causes. Smokers also argue that smoking bans trample on their individual rights.

Excise Taxes

Some antismoking advocates believe that charging an excise tax on tobacco products is the most effective way to keep young people from smoking. Studies consistently show that teens are more sensitive than adults to the price of tobacco products. One 2008 study showed that a 10 percent increase in the price of cigarettes reduces youth smoking by about 7 percent and overall cigarette consumption by about 4 percent. The money collected through excise taxes often is earmarked to pay for antismoking campaigns and tobacco control law enforcement.

Not everyone agrees that cigarette excise taxes are a good way to address smoking, however. More smokers are found among poorer Americans than wealthy ones. As a result, people with less income pay more of the taxes, which some people think is unfair. Also, people complain that the tax is not always spent on tobacco use prevention programs. Still others worry that the excise tax will encourage teens to replace cigarettes with chewing tobacco or cigars that are not subject to the tax.

Primary Source Quotes*

How Should Teen Smoking Be Regulated?

"States have done an extraordinary job over the last 10 years in helping us stem the illegal tobacco sales to minors. Together we are making great strides in protecting our children from the death and disability that accompanies tobacco use."

—Terry Cline, "Federal/State Program Achieves Dramatic Nationwide Drop in Tobacco Sales to Minors," SAMHSA, press release, October 11, 2007. www.samhsa.gov.

Cline is an administrator at SAMSHA, which monitors states' implementation of the Synar Amendment.

"A funny thing happened on the way to stamping out teen smoking: The more the nation learned about how to do it, the less some states have done."

—*USA Today*, "Our View on Anti-tobacco Campaign: States Slack Off on Snuffing Out Teen Smoking," editorial, July 2, 2008. http://blogs.usatoday.com.

USA Today is a daily newspaper with a large national audience.

Bracketed quotes indicate conflicting positions.

* Editor's Note: While the definition of a primary source can be narrowly or broadly defined, for the purposes of Compact Research, a primary source consists of: 1) results of original research presented by an organization or researcher; 2) eyewitness accounts of events, personal experience, or work experience; 3) first-person editorials offering pundits' opinions; 4) government officials presenting political plans and/or policies; 5) representatives of organizations presenting testimony or policy.

66 **One of the most effective ways countries can protect young people from experimenting and becoming regular tobacco users is to ban all forms of direct and indirect tobacco advertising, including promotion of tobacco products and sponsorship, by the tobacco industry, of any events or activities.** 99

—World Health Organization, "World No Tobacco Day 2008: Tobacco-Free Youth," May 31, 2008. www.who.int.

The coordinating authority for health within the United Nations, WHO provides leadership on global health matters.

66 **Banning sales sets up a virtuous cycle because younger kids see fewer and fewer older role models smoking cigarettes.** 99

—Joseph R. DiFranza, "Enforcing Bans on Cigarette Sales to Kids Reduces Youth Smoking," Substance Abuse Policy Research Program, press release, April 16, 2009.

DiFranza, a professor of family medicine and community health at the University of Massachusetts Medical School, is a leading authority on policy related to teen smoking.

66 **If it could be proven that tobacco causes people to kill their neighbors for the fun of it, it still would not be banned due to the massive taxes collected [from the sale of cigarettes].** 99

—Daryl Stanford, "Responding to Letter on Smoking: Letter to the Editor," *Waxahachie Daily Light*, July 9, 2009. www.thedailylight.com.

Stanford, who is trying to quit smoking, has called upon legislators to outlaw cigarettes.

66 **Increasing the legal age to 21 will just glorify the use of tobacco. Teens will have others buy it for them, just like they do for alcohol.** 99

—Alyssa Schmidt-Carr, "Raising Oregon's Smoking Age," Opinions, *Beacon*, April 16, 2009. http://media.www.upbeacon.net.

Schmidt-Carr is a student at the University of Portland in Oregon, where legislation has been proposed to raise the legal age for smoking to 21.

66 Our data indicate that improving merchant compliance with the prohibition on sales of tobacco to minors and increasing the price of cigarettes discourage youth smoking. 99

—Joseph R. DiFranza et al., "Enforcement of Underage Sales Laws as a Predictor of Daily Smoking Among Adolescents: A National Study," *BMC Public Health*, April 17, 2009.

DiFranza and the other writers of this report are researchers at the University of Massachusetts Medical School's Department of Family Medicine and Community Health.

66 Even though youth-access restrictions are taken more seriously now than they were a decade ago, there is still little evidence that increased retailer compliance has had a meaningful impact on the availability of tobacco to minors or that retailer compliance has had any independent effect in reducing the rates of youth smoking initiation or levels of cigarette consumption. 99

—Institute of Medicine, *Ending the Tobacco Problem: A Blueprint for the Nation.* Washington, DC: National Academies Press, 2007.

The Institute of Medicine provides independent, objective, evidence-based advice to policy makers, health professionals, the private sector, and the public.

66 The tobacco companies continue to be a significant barrier to the enactment of strong and effective tobacco control policies at the state and federal level. 99

—American Lung Association, "Executive Summary: State of Tobacco Control, 2008." www.stateoftobaccocontrol.org.

The American Lung Association seeks to improve lung health and prevent lung disease through researach, education, and advocacy.

66 Tobacco companies have the First Amendment right to express their opposition to laws and policies aiming to suppress tobacco use. 99

—Institute of Medicine, *Ending the Tobacco Problem: A Blueprint for the Nation.* Washington, DC: National Academies Press, 2007.

The Institute of Medicine provides independent, objective, evidence-based advice to policy makers, health professionals, the private sector, and the public.

Facts and Illustrations

How Should Teen Smoking Be Regulated?

- All **50 states have laws prohibiting the sale of tobacco products to minors**. At least 4 states have raised the minimum age to 19; several others have proposed legislation to raise the age to 19 or 21.

- Over **60 percent** of tobacco product sales occur at convenience stores.

- Minors are successful at buying tobacco products **60 to 90 percent** of the time and purchase over **1 billion packs** of cigarettes per year.

- According to the Institute of Medicine, more than **50 percent** of all youth smokers usually buy the cigarettes they smoke, either directly from retailers or vending machines or by giving money to others to buy cigarettes for them.

- Roughly **a third** of young smokers typically get their cigarettes from others (usually other kids) for free; a small but significant percentage of kids obtain their cigarettes **by shoplifting**.

- The Youth Risk Behavior Survey shows that **20 percent** of high school students usually purchase their cigarettes at a store or gas station. More boys than girls get their cigarettes in this way, and the percentage increases as students get older.

- **Fifty-seven percent** of eighth graders—13 or 14 years old—say they can get cigarettes "fairly easily" or "very easily," down from **77 percent** in 1996.

An Increasing Number of Cigarette Retailers Refuse Minors

Many experts believe that reducing access to cigarettes and other tobacco products is integral to reducing smoking among young people. Since the 1992 passage of the Synar Amendment, which required states to enact and enforce laws prohibiting the sale of tobacco products to minors, compliance with these laws has steadily increased. In 1997 over 40 percent of retailers were cited for violating laws restricting tobacco sales to minors, a decade later the retailer violation rate was under 11 percent. While these trends show great improvement, antismoking advocates argue that the 10.5 percent violation rate remains too high.

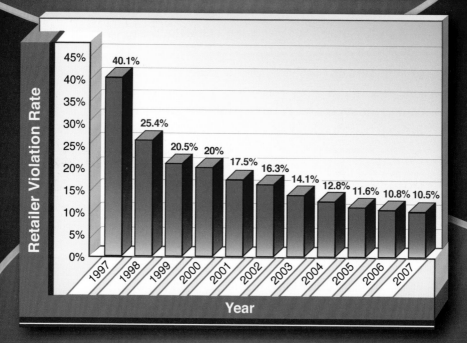

Note: All figures include data from the 50 states and the District of Colombia.

Source: Substance Abuse and Mental Health Services Administration, "Youth Tobacco Sales: FFY 2007 Annual Synar Reports," 2007. http://prevention.samhsa.gov.

• In a 2006 nationwide survey, **63 percent** of Americans said they support raising the minimum legal age to buy cigarettes from 18 to 21.

Teens Say Cigarettes Are Easy to Buy

Despite attempts to strengthen laws that restrict youth access to tobacco products, most teens say that cigarettes are easy to buy. The vast majority of teens under 18 years of age who smoke cigarettes say they usually buy them at a store or gas station. Fewer eighth and tenth graders say that cigarettes are "fairly easy" or "very easy" to get today than in the early 1990s. While antismoking activists are encouraged by this change, they say the fact that more than half of students report they can get cigarettes easily suggests that additional changes are needed.

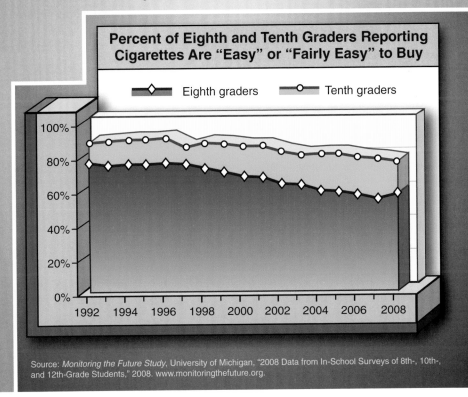

Percent of Eighth and Tenth Graders Reporting Cigarettes Are "Easy" or "Fairly Easy" to Buy

Source: *Monitoring the Future Study*, University of Michigan, "2008 Data from In-School Surveys of 8th-, 10th-, and 12th-Grade Students," 2008. www.monitoringthefuture.org.

- In a 2008 Massachusetts study, teens living in towns with restaurant smoking bans were **40 percent** less likely to become regular smokers than those in communities with no bans or weak ones.

- Stronger law enforcement from 1996 to 2003 led to a **20.8 percent** drop in the odds of tenth graders becoming daily smokers.

How Teens Get Cigarettes

This research undertaken by Philip Morris shows that teens are far more likely to get a cigarette from a friend or someone else than to purchase cigarettes for themselves. In fact, only 6 percent of teens 11 to 14 years old bought their own cigarettes. Younger teens are more apt than older teens to take a cigarette from someone else without asking—often from a parent or older sibling who smokes. Seventeen percent of 11- to 14-year-olds sneak cigarettes, compared to 6 percent of 15- to 17-year olds. It is common for minors to get someone else to buy cigarettes: almost one-quarter of teens 15 to 17 years old say this is how they have obtained their cigarettes. Some experts say this indicates that 18-year-olds are purchasing cigarettes for younger friends. Legislators have used this as an argument for raising the minimum age of purchase.

How Cigarettes Are Usually Obtained

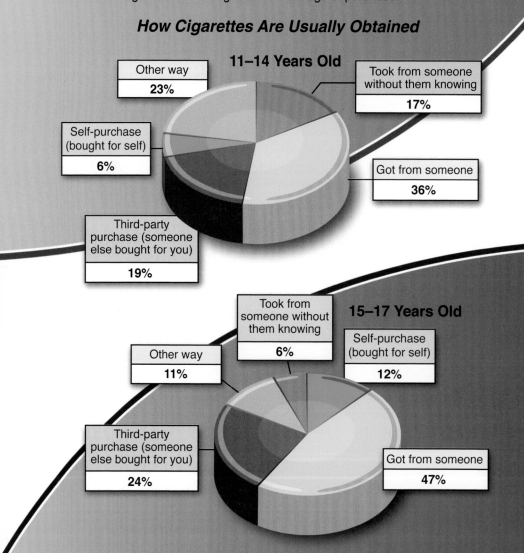

11–14 Years Old

Other way
23%

Took from someone without them knowing
17%

Self-purchase (bought for self)
6%

Got from someone
36%

Third-party purchase (someone else bought for you)
19%

15–17 Years Old

Took from someone without them knowing
6%

Other way
11%

Self-purchase (bought for self)
12%

Third-party purchase (someone else bought for you)
24%

Got from someone
47%

Source: Philip Morris USA Youth Tobacco Prevention, *Teenage Attitudes and Behavior Study, 2007 Results.* 2008.

Few Americans Think Smoking Should Be Illegal

Of all the ways of reducing smoking—among youth and young adults—outlawing cigarettes is consistently one of the least popular options. According to a Gallup poll, the percentage of Americans who support a ban on smoking rose slightly from 14 percent in 1990 to 17 percent in 2009. However, this group still represents less than a quarter of the American public.

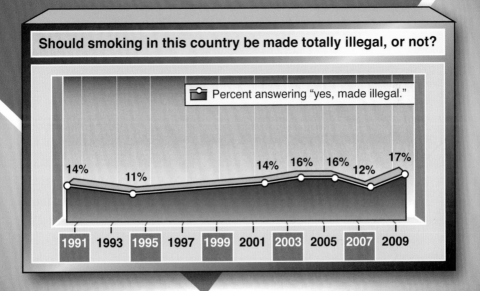

Should smoking in this country be made totally illegal, or not?

Percent answering "yes, made illegal."

14% | 11% | 14% | 16% | 16% | 12% | 17%

1991 1993 1995 1997 1999 2001 2003 2005 2007 2009

Source: Gallup Poll, "Majority Disapproves of New Law Regulating Tobacco," June 22, 2009. www.gallup.com.

- A 2009 study concluded that for every **1 percent** increase in the rate of compliance with laws prohibiting the sale of tobacco to minors, daily smoking among tenth graders fell **2 percent**.

- In a 2009 Gallup poll, **17 percent** of Americans said they were in favor of making cigarettes illegal.

- State excise taxes range from **$0.07** per pack in Georgia to **$3.46** in Rhode Island. The highest combined state-local tax rate on a pack of cigarettes is **$4.25** in New York City.

How Can Teen Smoking Be Prevented?

"Communitywide programs to counteract pro-tobacco marketing . . . should include combinations of counter-advertising mass media campaigns; comprehensive school-based tobacco-use prevention policies and programs; community interventions that reduce tobacco advertising, promotions, and commercial availability of tobacco products; and higher prices of tobacco products through increases in unit prices and excise taxes."

—Centers for Disease Control and Prevention, a U.S. agency charged with reducing illness and deaths.

"Few studies have evaluated the long-term impact of school-based smoking prevention programs rigorously. Among the programs that have follow-up data to age 18 or 12th grade, we found little to no evidence of long-term effectiveness."

—Sarah Weihe, researcher at Indiana University School of Medicine.

Regardless of whether it is a 13-year-old taking a puff of a cigarette for the first time, a 15-year-old who "only" smokes at parties, or a 17-year-old who switches to chewing tobacco because he thinks it is safer, teens quickly become hooked on tobacco. While these teens are experimenting, they are exposing themselves to a highly addictive drug. Antismoking activists believe that preventing kids from starting to smoke is the best way to reduce smoking-related health problems and their costs.

Mass Media Antismoking Campaigns

Government agencies and national organizations, including the Centers for Disease Control and Prevention and the American Lung Association, have embarked on aggressive media campaigns to educate young people about the risks of smoking. The campaigns have become increasingly hard-hitting over the years. Today's ads often attempt to capture attention with gruesome images and heart-wrenching stories of young people who have lost loved ones or died themselves from smoking-related illness. Recognizing that teens are often immune to messages about long-term health concerns, some antismoking campaigns focus on more immediate results, arguing, for instance, that smoking makes a teen physically unattractive and unpopular with the opposite sex.

Some recent campaigns portray the tobacco industry as a villain. Florida's "Truth" campaign, for instance, showed the tobacco industry accepting an award—along with Hitler and Stalin—for reaping so many deaths. An advertisement of the American Legacy Foundation in its national antismoking campaign portrays a group of teens piling up body bags outside the headquarters of a tobacco company while they announce through a megaphone that the bags represented the 1,200 people killed by tobacco each day.

Research shows that mass media messages can be an effective deterrent to teen smoking. Showing an antismoking clip prior to a movie has been shown to counteract—at least partly—the correlation between the portrayal of tobacco use during a

> " Today's [youth smoking prevention campaigns] often attempt to capture attention with gruesome images and heart-wrenching stories of young people who have lost loved ones or died themselves from smoking-related illness. "

> ## "
> All the large U.S. tobacco companies sponsor youth smoking prevention programs. Although their television advertisements are no longer shown, the tobacco companies issue antismoking brochures and sponsor school-based teen prevention programs. "

movie and youth smoking. An American Legacy Foundation study concluded that 2 percent fewer young people smoke because of the foundation's antismoking campaign.

Not all media antismoking efforts are the same, however. Some research suggests that the antismoking campaigns sponsored by tobacco companies do little to reduce teen smoking. In fact, researchers warn that these antismoking ads may actually contribute to an increase in smoking among young people. Antismoking campaigns of tobacco companies tend to blame peer pressure for teen smoking and portray tobacco use as an "adult" activity. Rarely (if ever) do tobacco company campaigns tell about the impact of smoking on health.

Speaking Out

From music trends to fashion styles to behaviors like smoking, children and teens often follow the behavior of celebrities they see in movies and on TV. As a result, nonprofit and government organizations often include movie stars and professional athletes as spokespersons. In 2001 actors Sean Penn, Jason Patric, Ted Danson, and other Hollywood stars teamed up with health care professionals in *Scene Smoking: Cigarettes, Cinema and the Myth of Cool*, a documentary about the influence of the portrayal of tobacco use in movies. Another project sponsored by the CDC's Office on Smoking and Health featured Jeremy London, a star of the teen hit TV show "Party of Five," in two 30-second antismoking advertisements. At the top of their career, music superstars Boyz II Men worked with the CDC in its campaign against tobacco called "Smoke-Free: It's the New Evolution."

Other musicians have banded together to insist that smoking be prohibited in the venues where they play. Fiona Apple, Tracy Chapman, and Rickie Lee Jones are among the many musicians who have requested nonsmoking shows. Queen made all concerts on its 2005 comeback tour smoke-free, and country legend Willie Nelson will only play in venues where smoking is prohibited.

Some musicians may be looking after their own interests: Second-hand smoke makes it difficult to sing. But the smoke-free requests of others are part of a conscious antismoking message. In the late 1990s, Leslie Nuchow, a struggling musician, turned down a lucrative deal with a record label when she learned that it was backed by the Virginia Slims cigarette company. "My music is the truest part of me," explains Nuchow, "and the thought of allowing it to be used by the tobacco industry to lure anyone, particularly young girls, into smoking is totally inconsistent with my values and what my music is about."[24]

> With older children, physicians' questions should go beyond inquiring about tobacco use in general to ask specific questions about teens' experiences with tobacco use by others.

Like entertainers and musicians, many sports stars have joined the antitobacco crusade. Baseball has for many years been associated with chewing tobacco. Some professional baseball players continue to chew tobacco, but others have joined efforts to publicize the dangers. New York Yankees shortstop Derek Jeter, Atlanta Braves' first baseman Andres Galarraga, and Cy Young Award–winning pitcher John Smoltz have all been involved in antismoking campaigns, as have football quarterbacks Troy Aikman and Steve Young. Skateboarder Tony Hawk has declined big-money offers from tobacco companies.

From Addiction to Prevention

Supermodel Christy Turlington's first experience with cigarettes is typical. Turlington says she smoked her first cigarette at 12 or 13; by 19 she was smoking more than a pack a day. "My father smoked for most of his life," says Turlington. "I really looked up to him and I honestly think that his smoking had an influence on my curiosity."[25]

Turlington tried to quit several times before succeeding—her father was not so lucky. He quit smoking just six months before he died of lung cancer in his early fifties. For Turlington, this was inspiration for activism: "After watching my father die of a disease that was a direct result of smoking . . . I decided right away that I would go out there and do my best in terms of prevention and awareness, especially among young people, because so much damage can be done in those early years of smoking."[26] The CDC hired Turlington for its antismoking commercials; Turlington also speaks about the dangers of smoking at schools and other venues and hosts the Web site SmokingIsUgly.com.

Tobacco Industry Prevention Programs

All the large U.S. tobacco companies sponsor youth smoking prevention programs. Although their television advertisements are no longer shown, the tobacco companies issue antismoking brochures and sponsor school-based teen prevention programs. The tobacco companies insist that such efforts are in good faith, but critics are skeptical. They claim that the goal of these programs is not to dissuade smoking but rather to improve the corporate image of the companies and to reduce opposition to smoking among the general public. Some critics also say that tobacco companies use the opportunity to gain information about teen preferences so they can create products that will appeal to young people.

School-Based Programs

Schools have implemented a variety of programs for preventing tobacco use by youths. Often these programs are incorporated into the health curricula of schools, starting with early elementary grades. Effective programs reach students again and again during their lives, with intense training during middle school, when students are most tempted to try their first cigarette.

While evidence suggests that school-based programs can achieve short-term success in preventing the initiation of smoking among young people, researchers have questioned their effectiveness over the long term. The best programs, say experts, are those that combine information about the health risks associated with smoking with life skills training that teaches students how to deal with stress and peer pressure.

Better still are programs that require students to take on an advocacy role. Some programs have students write letters to urge legislators to introduce or pass smoking bans or other antismoking legislation, for instance. Others have students participate in community action projects in which they gather stories of past smokers or work with people trying to quit. Research also shows that smoking prevention programs can have longer-term effects when they are combined with media and community programs.

The Role of Health Professionals

The medical profession plays an important role in prevention. Guidelines for health professionals recommend that pediatricians discuss smoking at annual checkups. While the inclination is to wait until early teens, when kids are most likely to try their first cigarette, health care professionals recommend initiating these conversations earlier; Madeline Dalton, a doctor specializing in smoking prevention, suggests starting to talk about tobacco use when children are just two or three years old.

With older children, physicians' questions should go beyond inquiring about tobacco use in general to ask specific questions about teens' experiences with tobacco use by others. If teens admit to smoking, doctors should gain information about frequency and about the impact that the tobacco use has on the teen's environment and relationships.

By opening a dialogue, physicians can begin to uncover risk factors among patients who might be tempted tobacco and, for those who have tried smoking, some of the reasons underlying their behavior. Physicians also should refer teen smokers to counseling services or community smoking cessation programs. The information gathered in routine checkups can also help provide physicians and others with information about how to prevent further tobacco use.

Can Parents Make a Difference?

One of the most important things that parents can do to minimize the risk of a child smoking is to not take up smoking themselves—or to quit if they do smoke. Research shows that children and teens are far more likely to smoke if parents or others in the household smoke. Parental disapproval of smoking also can be an important influence. Children and teens in homes where smoking was not allowed and who received strict punishments for breaking parents' antismoking rules to have a much lower incidence of smoking.

Many antismoking advocates also believe that active parenting can help reduce the risk of smoking. Children of parents who are actively involved in their lives—helping them with homework, attending their games and school events, and interacting with their friends—are less likely to smoke than those with more distant parents. Simply talking to one's child about the dangers of tobacco can also be a deterrent.

Positive Peer Pressure

Just as peers can influence teens to begin smoking, peer pressure can be used to dissuade students from smoking. Most students overestimate the number of teen smokers and assume peers have a more positive attitude toward tobacco use than they really have. The vast majority of teens say they disapprove of smoking and that they would not date someone who smoked. Studies show that teens who join a social group or club that promotes healthy living are less likely to smoke. In addition, schools in which participation on teams means no smoking have lower incidences of smoking than those without such rules.

> One of the most important things that parents can do to minimize the risk of a child smoking is to not take up smoking themselves—or to quit if they do smoke.

Capitalizing on peer pressure often means enlisting teens and young adults as spokespersons. Teens often are more effective than adults in capturing the attention of their peers and convincing youths that tobacco use is not only unhealthy but also "un-cool." Some schools have trained peer counselors who help students know how to resist the temptations to begin smoking.

Helping Teens Quit

Research shows that to become addicted to nicotine requires only a few cigarettes. Most teens think they can quit anytime, but very few actually succeed in doing so. Experts believe that helping teens quit smoking is an important element of a prevention program. Encouraging older teens to quit reduces the likelihood that younger teens will see someone smoking, which is important for preventing tobacco use before it starts. In addition, having older teens share stories about how hard it is to quit can be more influential than stories from parents or adults.

Experts say tobacco cessation programs for teens need to have a different focus than those for adults. Successful programs help teen smokers identify the reasons why they smoke and then look for alternatives to these factors. Behavioral strategies are critical. As with adults, these strategies teach patients how to handle cravings, the importance of avoiding situations in which they may be tempted to smoke, and preventing and handling relapses. Teens may also need coaching to resist peer pressure to start smoking again.

Smoking cessation programs are often overlooked, but experts say that they can be an important element of a successful prevention initiative. Multipronged prevention—and cessation—strategies balance information about the dangers of tobacco with skill-based training on making good decisions and dealing with peer pressure.

Primary Source Quotes*

How Can Teen Smoking Be Prevented?

> **More work still needs to be done to communicate the devastating health effects of tobacco use, because too many lives are still lost needlessly to smoking.**

—Quit, "Quit Calls for Bigger Graphic Health Warnings," January 19, 2009. www.cancervic.org.

Quit is a smoking cessation program of the Cancer Council Victoria, a Canadian nonprofit organization involved in cancer research and prevention.

> **Kids know what the effects of smoking are. We've come a long way in educating children about the dangers of smoking. Yet plenty of children start smoking every day. . . . I think smoking at their age has a lot more to do with peer pressure than being scared of the effects.**

—Steve Sands, "Helping Kids Say No to Peer Pressure: From Humor to Resisting Peer Pressure," Associated Content, December 2, 2008. www.associatedcontent.com.

Sands provides commentary on family and parenting issues for the Associated Content Web site.

Bracketed quotes indicate conflicting positions.

* Editor's Note: While the definition of a primary source can be narrowly or broadly defined, for the purposes of Compact Research, a primary source consists of: 1) results of original research presented by an organization or researcher; 2) eyewitness accounts of events, personal experience, or work experience; 3) first-person editorials offering pundits' opinions; 4) government officials presenting political plans and/or policies; 5) representatives of organizations presenting testimony or policy.

66 Peer pressure is one reason why adolescents are at much greater risk than adults for starting to smoke.99

—Lawrence Kutner, "Peer Pressure & Smoking," Youth Smoking Prevention, Philip Morris USA, 2008.

Kutner is codirector of the Harvard Medical School Center for Mental Health and Media and chairs the Philip Morris Youth Smoking Prevention program advisory board.

66 The more you hear about smoking, the more you want to try it. It doesn't really have anything to do with being cool.99

Lizzie, interview by author, June 16, 2009.

Lizzie, a 15-year-old smoker, tried her first cigarette at 13.

66 We believe the American public expects tobacco companies to help prevent kids from smoking or using any tobacco products. As the largest tobacco manufacturer in the U.S., we believe we should take a lead in this effort.99

—Philip Morris, "Youth Access Prevenition," PhilipMorrisUSA.com, June 2009. www.philipmorrisusa.com.

Philip Morris is the largest tobacco company in the world.

66 Philip Morris and the other tobacco companies should just stay away from our children.99

—Campaign for Tobacco-Free Kids, "New Study Finds Tobacco Industry 'Prevention' Ads Don't Work and Encourage Kids to Smoke," press release, October 31, 2006. www.tobaccofreekids.org.

The Campaign for Tobacco-Free Kids is a smoking prevention Web site that encourages activism to protect young people from the dangers of tobacco.

❝The smoking prevention ads broadcast by tobacco companies may not be reducing youth smoking, and ads aimed at parents may actually be encouraging youth in their middle and later teenage years to smoke.❞

—*American Journal of Public Health*, news release, October 31, 2006. www.ajph.org.

The *American Journal of Public Health* is a publication of the American Public Health Association.

❝It seems likely that some of the attitudinal change surrounding cigarettes is attributable to the adverse publicity suffered by the tobacco industry in the 1990s, as well as a reduction in cigarette advertising and an increase in antismoking advertising reaching children.❞

—Lloyd D. Johnston, *Monitoring the Future National Results on Adolescent Drug Use: Overview of Key Findings, 2008.* Bethesda, MD: National Institute on Drug Abuse, 2009.

Johnston is a lead researcher of the annual *Monitoring the Future* study.

❝It is plausible that parents can directly prevent their children from smoking by monitoring and restricting their activities, restricting their access to tobacco, and discouraging or disallowing their children from associating with peers who use tobacco.❞

—Institute of Medicine, *Ending the Tobacco Problem: A Blueprint for the Nation.* Washington, DC: National Academies Press, 2007.

The Institute of Medicine provides independent, objective, evidence-based advice to policy makers, health professionals, the private sector, and the public.

❝The greatest asset each school has in preventing nicotine addiction is its ex-smoking students, hooked students and those battling to break free.❞

—John R. Polito, "School Smoking and Nicotine Dependency: Students Helping Students," Why Quit on Youth? November 28, 2006. http://whyquit.com.

Polito is a nicotine dependency prevention and cessation educator and host of a smoking ceessation Web site.

How Can Teen Smoking Be Prevented?

- In SAMHSA's 2007 "Youth at Risk" survey, **41.5 percent** of teens who believed their parents did not "strongly disapprove" of smoking had smoked cigarettes in the previous month, compared to just **7.2 percent** of those who perceived strong parental disapproval.

- Over **75 percent** of high school seniors say that they prefer to date people who do not smoke, and nearly two-thirds agree with the opinion that "becoming a smoker reflects poor judgment."

- In SAMHSA's 2007 Youth at Risk survey, **89.7 percent** of youths "strongly" or "somewhat" disapproved of their peers smoking one or more packs of cigarettes per day.

- In a 2007 survey, **8.5 percent** of the teens who said their parents "always" or "sometimes" helped with homework were current smokers, compared with **16.3 percent** of those who indicated that their parents "seldom" or "never" helped.

- Teen smoking rates in states with aggressive programs declined more than the national average. After Maine began its antismoking campaign, for example, the rates of smoking declined **59 percent** among middle schools students and **48 percent** among high school students in just five years.

- Evidence suggests that effective school-based programs result in a **10 percent** reduction of smoking before age 24; combined with mass media or community programming these programs can reduce smoking by **20 percent**.

Cigarette Prices and Excise Taxes Vary Greatly

The price of cigarettes has a greater influence on whether teens begin smoking than most other factors. One of the main factors influencing cigarette prices is the excise tax. In addition to the federal cigarette tax ($1.01 per pack in 2009), all states have taxes on cigarette sales. These excise taxes vary greatly, from just 7¢ in Georgia to $3.46 in Rhode Island. (Rhode Island is the only state with a tax above $3.00.) As can be seen from the map, the "tobacco" states in the Southeast tend to have the lowest tax on cigarettes, while states in the Northeast have the highest taxes. The average tax rate is $1.27. States often earmark the funds raised through the sale of cigarettes for antismoking advertising and other prevention programs.

Legend:
- <$0.50
- $0.50–$0.995
- $1.00–$1.49
- $1.50–$1.99
- $2.00–$2.49
- >$2.50

Overall State Average: $1.27 per pack

Source: Campaign for Tobacco-Free Kids, "State Cigarette Excise Tax Rates and Rankings," May 28, 2009. www.tobaccofreekids.org.

- The Institute of Medicine predicts that ongoing education strategies can reduce the rate of smoking in America from **19.2 percent** in 2010 to **14.6 percent** in 2025.

Today's Teens Believe Smoking Carries Risks

Experts believe that perceived risk is associated with the use of any drug, including cigarettes. Data from the Monitoring the Future study show that more teens today perceive risks to be associated with smoking cigarettes than ever before. Almost three-quarters of high school seniors (74 percent) in 2008 said they believe that people who smoke one or more packs of cigarettes a day are at "great risk" of harming themselves.

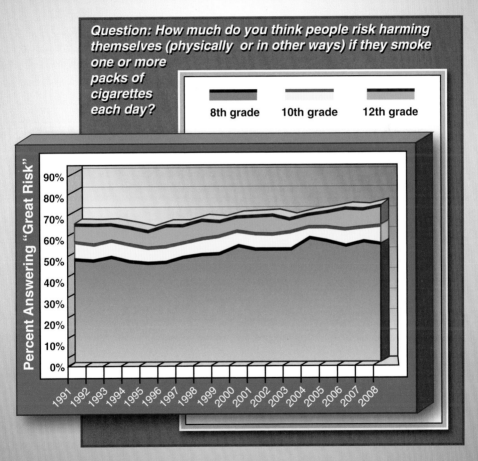

Source: Gallup Poll, University of Michigan, *Monitoring the Future National Results in Adolescent Drug Use: Overview of Key Findings, 2008.* National Institute on Drug Abuse, 2009.

- The Institute of Medicine predicts that enacting strong smoking prevention policies that include a **$2.00 increase** on the price of a pack of cigarettes could reduce the rate of smoking in America to **9.6 percent** in 2025.

Youth Smoking Rates by State

Youth smoking rates vary greatly from one state to another. States neighboring one another often have very different rates, as shown on this map. Experts believe that this may be due to state youth prevention initiatives that combine strong enforcement of tobacco control laws with youth education and school-based prevention programs. Some antismoking advocates have also been critical of the fact that much of the money given to states through the MSA settlement has not been used for prevention programs.

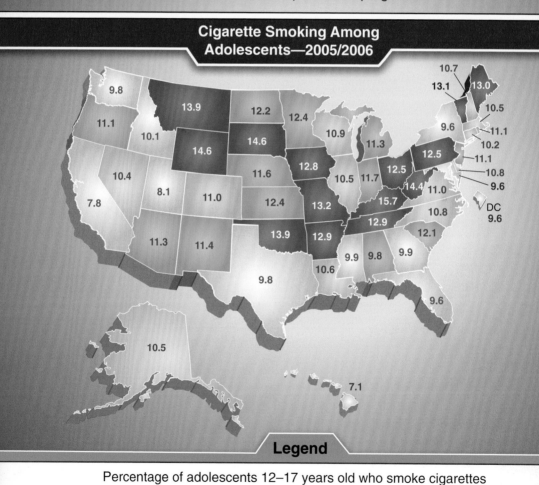

Cigarette Smoking Among Adolescents—2005/2006

Legend

Percentage of adolescents 12–17 years old who smoke cigarettes

- 7.11%–10.1%
- 10.2%–11.0%
- 11.1%–12.4%
- 12.5%–15.7%

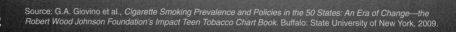

Source: G.A. Giovino et al., *Cigarette Smoking Prevalence and Policies in the 50 States: An Era of Change—the Robert Wood Johnson Foundation's Impact Teen Tobacco Chart Book.* Buffalo: State University of New York, 2009.

States Have Squandered Tobacco Prevention Funds

Some experts say that states are partly to blame for continued high rates of youth smoking because they have not used tobacco industry money provided through the 1998 Master Settlement Agreement for tobacco control and youth prevention activities. The settlement requires the tobacco companies to make annual payments to the states in perpetuity, with total payments estimated at $246 billion over the first 25 years. However, many states have used the funding to cover budget shortfalls and for other purposes. This map shows that only 9 states used 50 percent or more of the MSA funds for tobacco prevention programs.

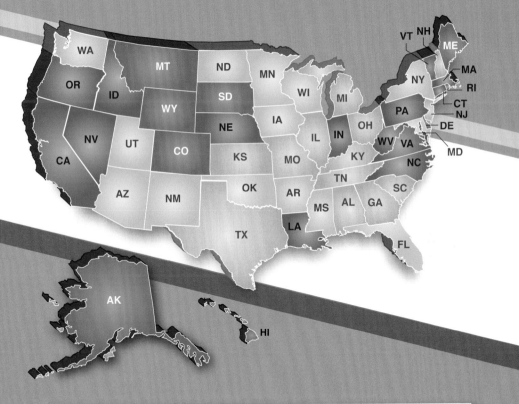

States that are spending 50% or more of CDC recommendation on tobacco prevention programs.

States that are spending 25%–49% of CDC recommendation on tobacco prevention programs.

States that are spending 10%–24% of CDC recommendation on tobacco prevention programs.

States that are spending less than 10% of CDC recommendation on tobacco prevention programs.

Source: Campaign for Tobacco-Free Kids, *A Decade of Broken Promises: The 1998 State Tobacco Settlement, Ten Years Later*, November 18, 2008.

- In the first year of Florida's antismoking media campaign, the rate of smoking among middle school and high school students dropped by **18 percent** and **8 percent**, respectively, which the CDC said was the largest annual reported decline observed in the United States since 1980.

- U.S. tobacco companies have spent millions of dollars on youth smoking prevention initiatives: Since 1999, Lorillard Tobacco Company has contributed more than **$80 million** to youth smoking prevention programs, and Philip Morris has spent over **$100 million** on its "Think. Don't Smoke" campaign and another **$125 million** in smoking prevention grants to schools and youth organizations.

- To address budget shortfalls, states have **cut back on funding for smoking prevention programs**. In 2009 Washington State lawmakers cut $22 million from tobacco prevention programs for the next 2 years; Maryland slashed funding for tobacco control from $16.7 million to $4.6 million; Colorado cut its tobacco education and cessation programs by $6 million.

- More than **80 percent** of high school seniors have been exposed to antismoking units as part of their school's health curriculum in middle and high school.

Key People and Advocacy Groups

American Cancer Society: The American Cancer Society provides a number of programs designed to prevent cancer, including conducting and publicizing research on the link between smoking and cancer and spearheading national antismoking programs.

American Legacy Foundation: Created from the proceeds of the 1998 Master Settlement Agreement, the American Legacy Foundation leads a number of programs to engage Americans in the dialogue about tobacco and to foster an understanding about its harmful effects, including the "Truth" advertising campaign.

American Lung Association: The American Lung Association's advocacy programs seek to influence the development and enforcement of laws and regulations related to lung health at the national, state, and local levels. The association provides authoritative information to policy makers.

Americans for Nonsmokers' Rights: This national lobbying organization has worked on behalf of nonsmokers' rights since 1974, focusing primarily on the dangers of secondhand smoke and supporting smoking ban initiatives.

Campaign for Tobacco-Free Kids: The Campaign for Tobacco-Free Kids encourages activism to keep tobacco products out of the hands of minors and provides information about federal and state initiatives to this end.

Centers for Disease Control and Prevention: The CDC engages in a wide range of programs to reduce illness and deaths in the United States and sponsors research on tobacco use among Americans of all ages.

Stanton Glantz: Glantz, a professor of medicine at the University of California Medical Center in San Francisco, has led several research projects into the dangers of smoking and wrote the 1998 book *The Cigarette Papers*. Glantz is an advocate of public health policies to reduce smoking. He is also one of the founders of the Americans for Nonsmokers' Rights organization and created the Web sites Smokefree Movies and Tobacco Scam.

My Smokers Rights: Sponsored by RJ Reynolds, My Smokers Rights defends the rights of smokers by providing information about local and state antismoking, smoke-free, and excise tax initiatives and urging smokers to write to legislators.

Philip Morris/Altria Group: Philip Morris, now called Altria Group, is the largest cigarette company in the world. Philip Morris works with other pro-tobacco organizations to protect the rights of tobacco companies to advertise, market, and distribute their products, including helping to draft proposed legislation.

Patrick Reynolds: A grandson of cigarette company founder RJ Reynolds, Reynolds first spoke out publicly at a congressional hearing in favor of a ban on all cigarette advertising in 1986; he has since spoken before dozens of municipal and state legislatures in support of cigarette tax increases, FDA regulation of tobacco, statewide smoking bans, and laws to limit youth access to cigarettes.

Smoking Lobby: The Smoking Lobby (Smokinglobby.com) is an online smoker's rights forum for both cigarette smokers and nonsmokers to discuss fundamental individual freedoms and the right to choose whether to smoke. The lobby is against smoking bans and believes that smoking is not nearly as harmful as portrayed by the media.

Christy Turlington: In 1997, after her father died of lung cancer, supermodel Turlington, a former pack-a-day smoker, lent her million-dollar looks to a series of antismoking public service announcements. She continues to speak out against smoking and hosts the Web site SmokingIs Ugly.com.

U.S. Surgeon General's Office: For half a century, surgeon general have publicized the risks of smoking to Americans. The Surgeon General's Office continues to be a major force for proposals to curb teen smoking.

Jeffrey Wigand: Wigand achieved national prominence in 1995 when he became the tobacco industry's highest-ranking former executive to address public health and smoking issues. He made the truth known to the public about the industry's disregard for health and safety during an interview with *60 Minutes* and during testimony against the tobacco companies. Wigand continues his efforts to reduce teen tobacco use through the nonprofit organization he formed, Smoke-Free Kids, Inc.

Chronology

1980
The Public Health Cigarette Smoking Act mandates warning labels be included on all packages of cigarettes.

1620s
John Rolfe and other Virginia settlers introduce tobacco to Europe.

1969
The Cigarette Smoking Act bans cigarette advertising on television and radio.

1998
The tobacco industry and states agree to the Master Settlement Agreement (MSA), prohibiting tobacco companies from targeting children and teens and imposing restrictions on tobacco advertising, marketing, and promotions.

1883
New Jersey and Washington become the first states to forbid the sale of tobacco products to minors.

1600   1800   1960   1980   2000

1964
The *Surgeon General's Advisory Committee Report on Smoking and Health* warns that tobacco use is linked to cancer and other diseases; the first warning labels are added to tobacco products.

1992
The Synar Amendment, included in the Alcohol, Drug Abuse, and Mental Health Reorganization Act, requires states to step up enforcement of laws prohibiting the sale of tobacco products to minors.

1967
Under the terms of the Fairness Doctrine, the Federal Communications Commision issues a ruling requiring stations airing cigarette commercials to also provide airtime for antismoking messages. This ushers in the first four-year decline in smoking rates in U.S. history.

2009
The Family Smoking Prevention and Tobacco Control Act, the first comprehensive antismoking law in decades, gives the Food and Drug Administration (FDA) oversight of the manufacture and distribution of tobacco and strengthens laws prohibiting the marketing of tobacco products to children.

Related Organizations

American Cancer Society

2200 Lake Blvd. NE

Atlanta, GA 30319

phone: (800) 227-2345

The American Cancer Society provides a number of programs designed to prevent and mitigate the effects of cancer, including research into the link between smoking and cancer and antismoking campaigns and literature.

American Legacy Foundation

1724 Massachusetts Ave. NW

Washington, DC 20036

phone: (202) 454-5555

Web site: www.americanlegacy.org

Created from the proceeds of the 1998 Master Settlement Agreement, the American Legacy Foundation leads a number of programs working to engage Americans in the dialogue about tobacco and to foster an understanding about its harmful effects, including the Truth advertising campaign, and advocates for the reduction of smoking in entertainment media.

American Lung Association

1301 Pennsylvania Ave. NW, Suite 800

Washington, DC 20004

phone: (800) 586-4872 or (212) 315-8700

Web site: www.lungusa.org

The American Lung Association offers a variety of smoking control and prevention programs for adults, school use, and home, including Teens Against Tobacco Use, a peer-teaching tobacco control program aimed at deterring young people from taking up smoking, and Not On Tobacco (N-O-T), a tobacco cessation program for teens.

Americans for Nonsmokers' Rights (ANR)

2530 San Pablo Ave., Suite J

Berkeley, CA 94702

phone: (510) 841-3032

Web site: www.no-smoke.org

Formed in 1976, Americans for Nonsmokers' Rights is a leading national lobbying organization dedicated to nonsmokers' rights. ANR pursues an action-oriented program of policy and legislation at all levels of government, protecting nonsmokers from exposure to secondhand smoke and preventing tobacco addiction among youth.

Campaign for Tobacco-Free Kids

1400 Eye St. NW, Suite 1200

Washington, DC 20005

phone: (202) 296-5469

Web site: www.tobaccofreekids.org

The Campaign for Tobacco-Free Kids encourages activism to keep tobacco products out of the hands of minors and provides information about federal and state initiatives to this end.

Centers for Disease Control and Prevention (CDC)

1600 Clifton Rd.

Atlanta, GA 30333

phone: (800) 232-4636)

e-mail: cdcinfo@cdc.gov • Web site: www.cdc.gov

CDC serves as the national focus for developing and applying disease prevention control and education activities designed to improve the health of Americans.

Foundation for a Smokefree America

PO Box 492028

Los Angeles, CA 90049-8028

phone: (800) 541-7741 or (310) 471-0303

Web site: www.anti-smoking.org

Sponsored by Patrick Reynolds, the Foundation for a Smokefree America's mission is to motivate youth to stay tobacco free and to empower smokers to quit. To achieve this mission, the foundation offers programs, fact sheets, and tips for adults and youth.

ImpacTeen

National Program Office

University of Illinois at Chicago

Institute for Health Research and Policy

1747 W. Roosevelt Rd., Room 558, M/C 275

Chicago, IL 60608

phone: (312) 413-0475 • fax: (312) 355-2801

Web site: www.impacteen.org

ImpacTeen is an interdisciplinary partnership of nationally recognized health experts with specialties in such areas as economics, etiology, epidemiology, law, political science, public policy, psychology, and sociology. The project, part of the Robert Wood Johnson Foundation's Bridging the Gap: Research Informing Practice and Policy for Healthy Youth Behavior, focuses on economic, environmental, and policy influences on youth substance use, obesity, and physical activity.

Substance Abuse and Mental Health Services Administration (SAMHSA)

1 Choke Cherry Rd.

Rockville, MD 20857

phone: (877) 726-4727 • fax: (240) 221-4292

Web site: www.samhsa.gov

This agency of the U.S. Department of Health and Human Services funds and administers a wide range of programs to address substance abuse among Americans. Through the Office of Applied Research, SAMSA also collects, analyzes, and disseminates national data on behavioral health practices and issues, including youth smoking.

Tobacco Control Network

Tobacco Technical Assistance Consortium

Rollins School of Public Health, Emory University

1520 Clifton Rd., SON 225

Atlanta, GA 30322

phone: (404) 712-8474

e-mail: ttac@sph.emory.edu

The Tobacco Control Network (TCN) comprises the tobacco control program managers and staff from each state, territory, and D.C. It provides advice and information to state and federal agencies and organizations involved in tobacco control.

For Further Research

Books

Jerald G. Bachman et al., *The Education–Drug Use Connection: How Successes and Failures in School Relate to Adolescent Smoking, Drinking, Drug Use, and Delinquency*. Mahwah, NJ: Lawrence Erlbaum, 2007.

Jane Bingham, *Smoking: What's the Deal?* Chicago: Heinemann Library, 2006.

Allan Brandt, *The Cigarette Century: The Rise, Fall, and Deadly Persistence of the Product That Defined America*. Cambridge, MA: Basic Books, 2007.

Sukhraj S. Dhillon, *Cigarette Smoking: What Its Doing to Smokers and Nonsmokers*. Dayton, OH: PPI, 2009.

Michael Rabinoff, *Ending the Tobacco Holocaust: How Big Tobacco Affects Our Health, Pocketbook and Political Freedom—and What We Can Do About It*. Santa Rosa, CA: Elite Books, 2007.

Frank A. Sloan et al., *The Price of Smoking*. Cambridge, MA: MIT Press, 2006.

Kenneth Warner, ed., *Tobacco Control Policy*. San Francisco: Jossey-Bass, 2006.

Rodger Williams, *Teen Smoking*. Detroit: Greenhaven, 2009.

Periodicals and Reports

Centers for Disease Control and Prevention, Office on Smoking and Health, "Sustaining Programs for Tobacco Control: State Data Highlights," 2006.

———, "Youth Risk Surveillance: United States, 2007," *Morbidity and Mortality Weekly Report*, June 6, 2008.

Institute of Medicine of the National Academies, *Ending the Tobacco Problem: A Blueprint for the Nation*. Washington, DC: National Academies Press, 2007.

Alan Mozes, "Smoking in Movies Linked to Kids Lighting Up," *U.S. News and World Report*, January 1, 2008.

National Cancer Institute, *The Role of the Media in Promoting and Reducing Tobacco Use,* Tobacco Control Monograph 19, June 2008.

Substance Abuse and Mental Health Services Administration, *Results from the 2007 National Survey on Drug Use and Health*, Office of Applied Studies, 2008.

———, "Youth Tobacco Sales," *FFY 2007 Annual Synar Reports*, 2008.

Linda Titus-Ernstoff et al., "Longitudinal Study of Viewing Smoking in Movies and Initiation of Smoking by Children," *Pediatrics*, January/February 2008.

Keilah A. Worth, Jennifer Duke, Molly Green, and James D. Sargent, "Character Smoking in Top Box Office Movies," *American Legacy Foundation First Look Report*, October 2007.

Films

Patrick Reynolds, *A Talk with Your Kids About Smoking: A Family DVD for Grades 6–12*. TobaccoFree.org, 2007.

Thank You for Smoking, 20th Century Fox, 2006.

Internet Sources

Americans for Nonsmokers' Rights, "U.S. Tobacco Control Laws." www.no-smoke.org/document.php?id=313.

Centers for Disease Control and Prevention, "Smoking & Tobacco Use." www.cdc.tobacco/index.htm.

———, "Youth Tobacco Prevention." www.cdc.gov/tobacco/youth/index.htm.

Federal Trade Commission, *Federal Trade Commission Cigarette Report for 2004 and 2005*, 2007. www.ftc.gov/reports/tobacco/2007 cigarette2004-2005.pdf.

Lloyd D. Johnston, Patrick M. O'Malley, Jerald G. Bachman, and John E. Schulenberg, *Monitoring the Future National Results on Adolescent Drug Use: Overview of Key Findings, 2008* (NIH Publication No. 09-7401). Bethesda, MD: National Institute on Drug Abuse, 2009. www.monitoringthefuture.org/pubs/monographs/overview2008. pdf.

U.S. Department of Health and Human Services, Centers for Disease Control and Prevention, Coordinating Center for Health Promotion, National Center for Chronic Disease Prevention and Health Promotion, Office on Smoking and Health, *The Health Consequences of Involuntary Exposure to Tobacco Smoke: A Report of the Surgeon General—Executive Summary*, 2006. www.surgeongeneral.gov/library/ secondhandsmoke/report/executivesummary.pdf.

Source Notes

Overview

1. Lloyd D. Johnston, Patrick M. O'Malley, Jerald G. Bachman, John E. Schulenberg, *Monitoring the Future, National Results on Adolescent Drug Use: Overview of Key Findings, 2008* (NIH Publication No. 09-7401). Bethesda, MD: National Institute on Drug Abuse, 2009, p. 7.
2. Centers for Disease Control and Prevention, "Youth Risk Behavior Surveillance—United States, 2007," *Morbidity and Mortality Weekly Report*, June 6, 2008. www.cdc.gov.
3. University of Michigan, "More Good News on Teen Smoking: Rates at or near Record Lows," press release, December 11, 2008. www.drugabuse. gov.
4. American Cancer Society, "Tobacco and Cancer." www.cancer.org.

How Serious a Problem Is Teen Smoking?

5. Quoted in "Teen Smoking Could Lead to Adult Depression, Study Says," press release, EurekAlert, January 29, 2009. www.eurekalert.org.
6. TeenGrowth.com, "Q&A Articles," June 5, 2002. www.teengrowth.com.
7. TeenGrowth.com, "Q&A Articles."

Who Is to Blame for Teen Smoking?

8. American Cancer Society, "Child and Teen Tobacco Use," October 3, 2008. www.cancer.org.
9. Quoted in Katy Abel, "Stamping Out Teen Smoking," *Family Education.* http://life.familyeducation.com.
10. Quoted in Abel, "Stamping Out Teen Smoking."
11. Quoted in Meg Riordon, "Tobacco Company Marketing to Kids," Campaign for Tobacco-Free Kids, September 30, 2008. www.tobaccofreekids. org.
12. Quoted in Riordon, "Tobacco Company Marketing to Kids."
13. Philip Morris USA, "Helping Reduce Underage Tobacco Use." www.philipmorrisusa.com.
14. National Cancer Institute, "The Role of the Media in Promoting and Reducing Tobacco Use," Tobacco Control Monograph 19, June 2008, p. 5.
15. Dan Glickman, "Film Rating Board to Consider Smoking as a Factor," press release, Motion Picture Association of America, Thursday, May 10, 2007. www.mpaa.org.
16. Smoke Free Movies, "The Problem: How Movies Sell Smoking." http:// smokefreemovies.ucsf.edu.
17. Philip Morris USA, "Marketing Our Cigarettes," 2009. www.philipmorris usa.com.
18. Philip Morris USA, "Marketing Our Cigarettes."

How Should Teen Smoking Be Regulated?

19. Quoted in Thomas Kaplan, "Bill Could Raise Smoking Age to 21," *Yale Daily News*, March 7, 2007. www. yaledailynews.com.
20. SAMHSA, *Youth Tobacco Sales, FFY 2007 Annual Synar Reports.* http:// prevention.samhsa.gov.
21. Institute of Medicine, *Ending the Tobacco Problem: A Blueprint for the Nation.* Washington, DC: National Academies Press, 2007, p. 210.
22. Scott T. Leatherdale and Steve Manske, "The Relationship Between Student

Smoking in the School Environment and Smoking Onset in Elementary School Students," *Cancer Epidemiology Biomarkers & Prevention*, July 2005. http://cebp.aacrjournals.org.

23. John R. Polito, "School Smoking and Nicotine Dependency: Students Helping Students," Why Quit on Youth? November 28, 2006. http://whyquit.com.

How Can Teen Smoking Be Prevented?

24. SLAM! "Leslie Said No." http://slammusic.tripod.com.
25. SmokingIsUgly.com, "Interview with Christy Turlington." www.smokingisugly.com.
26. SmokingIsUgly.com, "Interview with Christy Turlington."

List of Illustrations

Index

About the Author

Lydia D. Bjornlund is a writer in northern Virginia, where she lives with her husband, Gerry Hoetmer, and their wonderful children, Jake and Sophia. Bjornlund has written approximately 15 nonfiction books for children and teens, mostly on American history and health-related topics. She also writes books and training materials for adults on issues related to conservation and public management. Bjornlund holds a master's degree in education from Harvard University and a BA from Williams College.